D0886629

BUILDING the PERFECT FIRE

With or Without Matches in Any Weather

MILES TANNER

BLACK DOG
& LEVENTHAL
PUBLISHERS
NEW YORK

Black Dog & Leventhal Publishers
Hachette Book Group
1290 Avenue of the Americas
New York, NY 10104

www.hachettebookgroup.com
www.blackdogandleventhal.com

First Edition: May 2019

Black Dog & Leventhal Publishers is an imprint of Running Press, a division of Hachette Book
Group. The Black Dog & Leventhal Publishers name and logo are trademarks of Hachette Book
Group, Inc.

The publisher is not responsible for websites (or their content) that are not owned by the publisher.

The Hachette Speakers Bureau provides a wide range of authors for speaking events. To find out
more, go to www.HachetteSpeakersBureau.com or call (866) 376-6591.

Print book interior design by Paul Barrett
Produced by Girl Friday Productions

Image credits: 14, Alex Rockheart/Shutterstock; 18, Harry Bates; 21, Bodor Tivadar/Shutterstock;
24, Harry Bates; 26, white snow/Shutterstock; 28, Harry Bates; 30, LEOcrafts/Getty Images;
31, Harry Bates; 32, Bodor Tivadar/Shutterstock; 36, Harry Bates; 40, Harry Bates; 41, Harry
Bates; 44, Harry Bates, 47, Harry Bates; 48, Bodor Tivadar/Shutterstock; 53, Harry Bates; 55,
vectorisland/Shutterstock; 57, patta12/Shutterstock; 59, nikiteev_konstantin/Shutterstock; 60,
ambassador806/Getty Images; 62, Harry Bates; 70, Golden Shrimp/Shutterstock; 72, Harry Bates;
75, FrankRamspott/Getty Images; 77, Bodor Tivadar/Shutterstock; 82, ArtMari/Shutterstock; 86,
Harry Bates; 93, Bodor Tivadar/Shutterstock; 94, BORTEL Pavel - Pavelmidi/Shutterstock; 97,
Alexander_P/Shutterstock; 101, zhekakopylov/Shutterstock; 102, alongzo/Shutterstock; 104, Bodor
Tivadar/Shutterstock; 114, tigerstrawberry/Getty Images; 117, FrankRamspott/Getty Images

LCCN: 2018961627
ISBNs: 978-0-7624-9398-2 (paper over board), 978-0-7624-9397-5 (ebook)

Printed in China

1010

10 9 8 7 6 5 4 3 2 1

Dedicated to all those willing
to coax sparks into a flame.

Contents

Who has smelled the woodsmoke at twilight, who has seen the campfire burning, who is quick to read the noises of the night?

RUDYARD KIPLING

Foreword

Fire symbolizes passion and purity, creativity and motivation, mourning and regeneration. Through its unique capability for creation and destruction, fire is an element we've had to master, as our use and control of it has long set us apart as a species. Fire has kept us warm, made cooking food possible, and facilitated agriculture. Harnessing the heat from fire helped us to forge instruments that eased daily life and weapons for hunting and for fighting our enemies. Food cooked over fires changed our very anatomy, and artifacts hardened by fire became some of the earliest forms of art.

While fire still plays a critical role in the survival of much of the population, we're often further removed from it and less reliant on it in our daily lives. Despite our relative distance from fire nowadays, it still holds a special power that brings us together. There's nothing quite like watching a fire, while bathed in the glow of a dancing flame, hands held close to capture its warmth, as we are transfixed by the unique hold fire maintains over us.

And whether you build a fire to cozy up inside a mountain cabin, warm yourself at camp, or prepare the perfect backpacking meal, learning to create and extinguish fire is a worthy skill. This book is, in many ways, an invitation to explore an inherent, deeply rooted curiosity and to use the knowledge you gain in the process to enjoy one of life's greatest pleasures: a fire.

Introduction

I have always been fascinated by fire. As a child, I would sit by the fireplace and watch the flames as they consumed wood. Its mesmerizing qualities completely captured my attention. I loved the look, the smell, the sound of fire—I still do.

As a teen, I learned that a campout was not a campout without a roaring fire. We sat around it and talked, sang, ate, and just stared into the dazzling light show that both warmed us and lit our night.

I read about Native Americans of the Plains, marveling at their ability to eke fire from wood. Using Larry Dean Olsen's *Outdoor Survival Skills*, I began to practice making fire with pieces of wood that I collected and shaped into a bow and drill. After a few hundred attempts, I was finally able to create a flame from pieces of wood and my own muscle power. My study of fire had begun.

I hope the many lessons in this book inspire you to see your ability to control fire as a lifelong skill, one that our ancestors used to forge our world and one we still use today.

1

The Root of Civilization

×

Fire: An Essential Element
of the Human Experience

"The spread of civilization may be likened to a fire: first, a feeble spark, next a flickering flame, then a mighty blaze, ever increasing in speed and power."

Nikola Tesla

F ire is such a fundamental part of our daily life, and yet we often take it for granted. Pistons fire in our car engines to get us to work, pilot lights keep the flames of our natural gas heaters burning, gas ranges heat water for our morning coffee, and wood-burning stoves and campfires warm us from the inside out.

Our relationship with fire goes way, way back. And fire itself existed well before we came to rely on it. Although the source of Earth's earliest fire isn't known, a small, charred, leafless plant from nearly 420 million years ago is the earliest proof of fire's existence. When conditions on Earth nearly 345 million years ago created an environment that could support woody plants and contained enough oxygen to sustain them, wildfires that resemble those we know today began to burn. When atmospheric conditions allowed for the growth of vast savannas, major fires spread.

Scholars still debate when humans began using fire with regularity; the Wonderwerk Cave in South Africa may be one of the earliest sites of regular fire use by *Homo erectus*. But hard proof dates back to 300,000 to 400,000 years ago. In Israel, the Qesem Cave harbors evidence of the repeated use of a single hearth, where early humans roasted meat.

The adoption of fire changed the course of history. It enabled more advanced tools, extended our days, facilitated agriculture, and altered diets. The pattern of our days was no longer dictated by the sun's rise and fall; the light and warmth of fire allowed us to work and socialize deep into the night and to rise before dawn. Through cooking and smoking, fire allowed us to eat more meat and protein. It enabled us to forge sturdy tools, like pots, that increased our ability to store, cook, and carry food and water. As they still do, fires kept predatory animals and biting insects at bay. In addition to improving the everyday life of ancient people, fire became a mainstay of many religious and spiritual practices.

As one of the four classic elements, fire, with its ability to both create and destroy, is often a key element in many of the world's religious beliefs. The ancient Greeks told the story of Prometheus, who stole fire from the gods to give to man, thus creating civilization. A similar story was told by the Cherokee, with the role of fire giver

A SACRED BLAZE

In Zoroastrianism, one of the world's oldest religions, fire represents God's light or wisdom. Sacred blazes are maintained in Fire Temples and are part of all of their rituals and ceremonies.

being played by Grandmother Spider, while Hindus told a tale about the hero Mātariśvan.

This gift of the gods is still worshipped in many religions today. In Zoroastrianism, one of the world's oldest religions, no ritual is performed without the presence of fire, a symbol of their god and the illuminated mind. And many other religions regard fire with reverence and hold it as a mainstay of religious practices. Candles are lit at many Christian ceremonies, where the flame represents the Holy Spirit. Christians also believe the awesome power of fire will consume the world in its fiery end. The Jewish holiday of Hanukkah involves lighting the nine candles (eight candles plus the shammash, the candle used to light the others) of the menorah to commemorate the miracle of the candle that burned for eight days. Many of the old religions focused heavily on the sun's role in daily life, and though they regarded the sun as the Big Kahuna, the candles and lamps and altar fires were often symbols of the being who so profoundly affects all life on Earth.

Both symbolically and practically, fire is integral to our world. My goal with this book is to teach you to use fire in your world, both indoors and out.

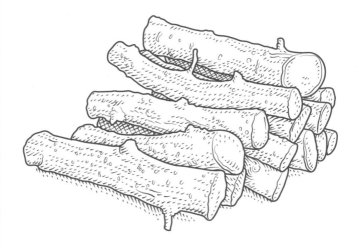

2

Considerations for Building the Fire

——— ✕ ———

Essentials to Keep in Mind

"A mighty flame followeth a tiny spark."

Dante Alighieri

Picture candles illuminating a feast at a dining table, laughter filling the room; a family snuggled on the couch in front of the living room fireplace; or faces huddled close to a flickering campfire, the brightest light under a starry sky. Fires draw people together. And if you're out camping alone, fires provide welcome comfort. Fires also dry clothes wet from rain, warm hands cold from snow, and cook coffee or soup. Through both their utilitarian and more ethereal functions, fires have a unique power to make everything good again.

And fires come with responsibility. We'll make our way to learning where and how to build an ideal fire, but first, some safety tips.

FIRE SAFETY

Whether building your fire inside or out, safety is absolutely the most important consideration. Outdoors, when it comes to building a campfire, safety considerations mean being strategic about the location (foundation) and materials (fuel) that you use for your fire. When

IT'S OUR RESPONSIBILITY

Once there was a popular slogan made famous by Smokey Bear: "Remember, only YOU can prevent forest fires." Fires in the forest are generally regarded as a bad thing, especially if your home is about to go up in flames. So the policy has been to suppress fires. No one wants to lose their home—or their whole neighborhood! On the other hand, fire plays a critical role in both balancing and creating landscapes across the globe. In fact, many of the pine forests throughout the United States have historically experienced much more regular fires, with some forest types burning as often as every five to seven years. Fires clear the trees and shrubs that grow between the canopy and forest floor and establish habitats for many species. Many plants do not sprout up except after a fire. Fire is not a bad thing. It just is.

camping, make sure to check the posted rules in your area, as many municipalities prohibit open fires during spells of dry weather or drought in order to prevent forest fires. Inside, good fire safety could mean ensuring you're using the proper fuel, that you have adequate ventilation, and that you take the correct precautionary measures to keep your chimney clean. In each section of this chapter, we'll touch on good safety practices. But always remember to use common sense when working with fire.

When building a fire indoors, some important tools to have on hand for starting, maintaining, and extinguishing a fire are a metal poker, a shovel, and some sort of tin for removing ashes. Multiple fire extinguishers are necessary in case a fire gets out of hand. While fire extinguishers generally last between five and fifteen years, it's a good idea to have yours serviced regularly to ensure it's ready for you if you need it.

WHERE TO BUILD A FIRE

Much like real estate, building a successful fire is all about location, location, location. The most important factor in choosing the location of your fire—whether inside or out—is safety.

When it comes to building a fire outdoors, you're likely to rely on a fire ring—something designed to keep fires contained and temper

While it's lovely to have your tent near a campfire, always make sure your fire is at a safe distance. Many tents are flammable.

the impact of inclement weather on your flames. Fire rings can take many forms, but they're always floorless—that is, built directly on the ground. To make the ring, you can use rocks, metal, concrete, or other nonflammable/heat-resistant materials. In established campsites where fires are permitted, you'll likely find existing fire rings that you can use. Elsewhere, like your backyard or a primitive campground, you'll need to build your own.

If you're building a fire in a place without a fire ring, here are a few things to consider.

First: proximity. While the idea of a campfire right outside the flap of your tent may seem romantic, many of the materials used for older tents and sleeping bags are flammable. Many modern materials are fire-resistant but not fireproof and, at a minimum, are easily burned by embers. If possible, place your tent or shelter upwind of the fire and no closer than ten feet from it.

Second: foundation. Don't build the fire ring on thick duff—that soft, spongy layer on the forest floor made of decomposing leaves, sticks, and other organic materials. The ground should be flat and compact. Prepare the area by clearing a three-foot circle of all leaves, grass, and brush to the bare ground. Then, add a layer of dirt three to four inches thick.

Third: what's overhead. Look up and around you. Ensure there are no trees or shrubs hanging overhead or within a ten-foot radius.

BUILDING A FIRE INSIDE

When it comes to making a fire indoors, the questions of where to build your fire and what its foundation will be are already answered (fireplace, woodstove, etc.). But there are still important factors to consider. Any fireplace should have a good grate, a screen for errant sparks, and a working flue that lets smoke escape and ensures proper ventilation. Annual cleanings of your chimney are a good way to ensure proper airflow and avoid dangerous chimney fires.

WHAT DO YOU NEED TO MAKE A FIRE?

Now that you've covered your bases when it comes to safety, and you have your foundation picked out—your fire ring constructed or your chimney cleaned—it's time to build your fire.

Fire joins earth, air, and water as the fourth critical element considered fundamental to our existence. Much like water, each molecule of which can be broken down into two parts hydrogen and one part oxygen, fire is made of parts. The three essential ingredients for starting and maintaining a fire are heat, fuel, and oxygen.

HEAT

Heat to ignite a fire can come from a variety of sources. In nature, heat for fire is provided by things such as lightning strikes or the flow of lava. The heat that will light a match comes from friction. Ancient cultures also often used friction, such as spinning a drill against a piece of wood to create high temperatures and promote ignition. Once a fire is burning, the heat produced by the chemical reaction will cause other materials (hopefully, the additional wood in your fire) to combust.

FUEL

Fuel is anything that heat will ignite and flames will consume, which includes a broad diversity of materials. In nature as well as in our homes, we're usually talking about burning wood and other plant materials. When you're starting a fire, you'll want to think about fuel in three stages: tinder, kindling, and fuel. These categories can be broken down even further, but the critical piece is understanding that tinder requires the least exposure to heat in order to light (that is, it's the most flammable), which is why you'll start with tinder when lighting your fire (indoors or out). Kindling, especially small or fine kindling, should light fairly easily. Larger fuels will require longer exposure to heat in order to light, but once they do, they burn longer and hotter than tinder or kindling.

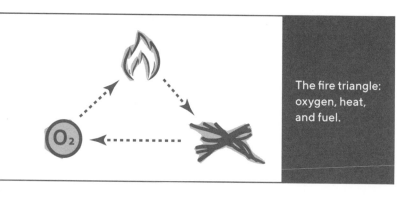

The fire triangle: oxygen, heat, and fuel.

Choosing the right fuel is a safety consideration as well. For indoor fires or wood-burning stoves, consider burning hardwoods. They burn hotter and cleaner than other types of fuel. A cool-burning fire with a lot of debris creates creosote, a combination of chemicals formed from unburned fuels. Over time, creosote can build up on the walls of your chimney and lead to a chimney fire.

OXYGEN

Oxygen is necessary for the fuel to burn. If you remove oxygen from a fire, it will be extinguished. The air around you is generally composed of approximately 21 percent oxygen, and fires require at least 16 percent oxygen to exist. Have you ever watched a camper blow on his campfire to get it going? He's giving it oxygen. When we exhale, the air we produce contains about 16 percent oxygen.

When it comes to extinguishing a fire, these three ingredients come into play again. Remove any one of them and your fire will cease to burn.

In the coming chapters, you'll learn how to build (and extinguish) a fire using these three key ingredients.

3

Heat

—— × ——

Matches, Lighters, and
Less Common Fire Starters

> *"The fire is the main comfort of the camp, whether in summer or winter, and is about as ample at one season as at another. It is as well for cheerfulness as for warmth and dryness."*
>
> Henry David Thoreau

Whether you're in your home or headed deep into the woods, it pays to have the appropriate tools and know the right methods for starting a fire. At home, this might mean being sure to have your matches stocked and a few lighters lying around. When you travel into the backcountry, you should carry the tools for getting a fire started in several ways. Matches are the most convenient. But remember, matches might run out or get wet, so you need to have a few other options as well.

MATCHES

Sulfur-based matches were invented by the Chinese in the sixth century AD. But the modern self-igniting matches weren't widely produced until the late 1800s. Our modern match is the result of various chemical combinations that are affixed to a wood stick or paper that, when rubbed onto something akin to fine sandpaper, bursts into a flame. When you use a match, you are utilizing two of

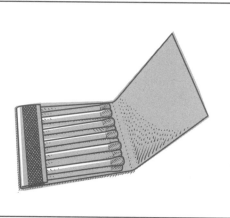

the principles by which fire is made: fuel (the chemicals) and heat (friction).

In general, wood matches are preferable to paper matches when you are lighting fires outdoors. Paper matchbooks, while common, degrade quickly and are unreliable in bad weather, so it is best not to count on them. In my early years of backpacking, I always carried ordinary wood matches, which I wrapped in tinfoil and stored in a canister or jar. When I needed to light a fire, I wanted my matches to work. As long as they were dry, I could count on them.

For ordinary wood matches, you need a proper striking surface, unless you buy the less common strike-anywhere matches. Without the right striking surface, you can go through many matches before you get a flame. It's a good idea to store a piece of very fine sandpaper with your fire gear in case your matchbox gets wet or damaged.

An even better option is to waterproof your matches so they still light in wet conditions. You can buy them online or in camping stores, often already in a waterproof container. They are well worth the extra cost over wood matches. These matches have a larger head, and when struck, flame for up to ten seconds before burning the wood, giving you more time to light your tinder.

LONG MATCHES

Home supply stores also sell extra long wooden matches for starting your barbecue or home fireplace. These are an excellent way to get some reach into the fire without having to stick your hand right in

Wooden matches are often made of white pine or aspen, then soaked in ammonium phosphate, which is a fire retardant. The tip combines two chemicals that ignite with friction and provide oxygen needed for combustion.

the middle of everything. These matches are often a foot or longer and well worth it from both a safety and a practicality standpoint.

BUTANE LIGHTER

Always carry an inexpensive butane lighter, such as a BIC. It's easy to bring a few with you wherever you go. Each one is good for a few hundred lights, and they're pretty reliable, unless the case gets cracked or you run out of fuel. But even then, they are not useless.

An empty lighter should still be able to produce a spark. If you place ideal tinder such as cotton or shredded cedar bark in front of the spark, you should be able to get a flame. So even an out-of-fuel butane lighter is useful for making a fire.

ATOMIC OR PLASMA BEAM LIGHTER

Besides a butane lighter, you can also buy an atomic or plasma beam lighter. Rather than using any fuel, you plug it into a USB port and

The first flint lighter was created by the Ronson company in 1913. This lead to the creation of first automatic flint lighter by the company in 1926. Butane wasn't used until the 1940s.

charge its battery. When you press a button, two ports produce a plasma beam strong enough to light your tinder, even in the wind. The downside is that you need an electrical outlet to recharge it. If you're ingenious, you can find a way to hook it up to a little solar panel and recharge it with the sun!

TINDER

In the oxygen + heat + fuel equation, tinder is the kind of material you'll want to capture the spark and coax it into flame. You should have a good supply at the ready when you're starting a fire. Tinder comes in many forms, from dryer lint to tree bark, and should catch fire easily and burn fast. Finding the right tinder is essential for starting a fire.

THE VALUE OF A CANDLE

On one of my earliest backpacking trips, I was accompanied by members of a local search and rescue team. When it came time to light a fire that night, I was having a hard time getting the fire going with my matches. So one of the rescuers showed me a trick. With a smile, he pulled a fat little pink candle out of his pack and lit it. With one match, his candle was lit. He let the candle wax drip all over the moist sycamore leaves, bay leaves, and pine needles I had such trouble lighting. Lo and behold, the tinder began burning. And the little flame dried out the other tinder. He moved the candle to the opposite side of the fire and did the same, creating a hot spot there too. We nurtured the spot by carefully laying pine needles all around its perimeter, and then adding little twigs, which quickly dried out. We continued this way until we had a roaring fire.

That fire provided us with plenty of warmth, coals for cooking, and a focal point as we sat around it and talked into the night. And I never forgot that little candle, and I always have one in my pack now.

Outdoor examples of material you can find are dry wood shavings, leaves, bark (especially birch), ferns, and grass, but they need to be dry to work. Dryer lint is a commonly recommended fire starter and, while it's convenient and *can* work, the materials that make up the lint (cotton, polypropylene, denim, dog hair, etc.) impact its flammability. Instead of taking the risk, try packing cotton balls coated in petroleum jelly, which can burn longer than dryer lint. Add a few extra cotton balls, which are also flammable—and they can double as first aid supplies. And, in a pinch, if your boots are rubbing you the wrong way and you're developing a blister, rub the area with the petroleum-coated cotton ball for some relief.

Another handy fire starter you can make at home is the pocket bottle-cap candle. It weighs a bit more than the cotton balls, and there is waste to cart out (the caps), but you won't need many and the flame lasts awhile. To make them, simply heat some candle wax in a pan and pour the wax into bottle caps. Cut candlewicks into inch-long strips and, once the wax begins to dry, insert two or three wicks in each cap. If you are short on time, votive candles work just as well.

Natural fire starters that might surprise you (and could come in handy in a pinch) include dry cattail fuzz, old-man's beard (hanging lichen found on the limbs of some coniferous trees), conifer resin, and spruce tips. Both spruce tips and conifer resin (found where branches have broken off or beetles have burrowed) require prolonged flame to catch but, once they do, will burn for a long time.

If you're camping in or near a dense forest, bring a waterproof container with you while you walk around to collect tinder. Tinder in well-traveled campsites may be hard to find, and tinder in the desert or high-alpine areas can be much trickier to come by, so packing your own is a fail-safe route. Plus, in some places, collecting tinder is

HOMEMADE FIRE STARTERS

Homemade fire starters became a part of our holiday traditions when I was young. In the midst of making cookies, my mom would cart a giant trash bag full of sawdust into the kitchen. She would lay it on the floor, fold the top open, and stick a measuring cup inside. Then she'd hand my brother and me a couple of packages of uncolored tissue paper (doubles for wrapping gifts) and some ribbon. On the stove, she would warm a pot of paraffin wax (available at most grocery stores). My brother and I would get to work cutting the tissue paper into 6" x 6" squares, putting a quarter cup of sawdust in the middle, wrapping the edges together, and tying the little package in a bow. My mother would dip our creations in wax and leave them to dry. They not only worked as excellent fire starters but also made great gifts.

You can take the creativity up a whole 'nother step by placing paper muffin cups into a tin and filling each with a short candlewick, a couple of small pine cones, acorns, bay leaves, and cinnamon sticks. Pour candle or paraffin wax into the muffin containers, let them dry, and voilà: fire starters that smell great, work well, and make a nice gift.

highly discouraged because it can quickly alter or damage the landscape due to overgathering. The organic matter that makes up tinder is vital to the health of the forest floor, so removing it entirely can disrupt the ecosystem's balance. That's why some high-use areas restrict or limit the gathering of tinder and firewood.

When it comes to lighting your fireplace or woodstove, fire starters come in a wide variety of shapes, sizes, and materials. Newspaper is a common source, but be careful to burn only the black-and-white newsprint. Color and glossy pages can produce toxic chemicals when burned.

Most hardware and convenience stores offer their own unique brand of fire starters, like Cabela's Magic Fire Starter. The thing is, even most fire starters sold in stores are easy to make at home.

USING THE SUN AS A FIRE STARTER

Whether in the movies or through your own experience, you've probably seen people put the sun's heat to work to start a fire. While the sun isn't always a reliable source (especially if you're camping in parts of the Northwest or Northeast), its light can be harnessed when necessary. By focusing sunlight through a lens, such as a magnifying glass, or bouncing it off of a reflector, such as a parabolic dish, you can concentrate light and transform it into heat for catching tinder. Here are a few options for using the sun to start fire.

THROUGH A LENS

In addition to the strength of the sunlight, two factors will play a significant role in the success or failure of your lens-to-flame efforts. The first is having ideal tinder prepared. Because the heat produced through this method isn't as strong as a flame, you'll want tinder that lights especially easily so you can coax your little sparks into a flame.

Second, you'll want to brace your arm to keep it still. Steady the lens perpendicular to the sun so that the light shines directly through the lens onto your tinder. If it works, on a sunny day you'll get a fine point of light, and your tinder will start smoking fairly quickly.

Using a lens to magnify the sun's rays and directing the light onto tinder is one possible way to start a fire.

To be safe, wear sunglasses when you try using a lens this way because the focal point of the light can be very bright. The focused sunlight can burn skin, so be sure to place the tinder on the ground or a rock while getting it to light.

TYPES OF LENS

While magnifying glasses are the most efficient, due in large part to their convex shape, they can be cumbersome to carry around.

PIGGY'S SPECS

Did you ever read *Lord of the Flies*? A plane crashes on an island, all the adults die, and a group of young boys have to survive on their own. The boys learn to start a fire with the eyeglasses of one of the boys, whom they called Piggy.

Fortunately for Piggy (and the others) he was farsighted, which is corrected with converging lenses, which bend the light toward a focal point. But farsighted lenses alone won't necessarily work to start a fire in real life. To enhance your odds, you'll need water. A drop of water in the middle of an eyeglass lens will bend the light and turn your glasses into a magnifying glass, helping to light a fire. Because they are magnifiers, common reading glasses will also work to start a fire.

Lenses used to correct nearsightedness, however, won't offer the same success. They are diverging, which means they bend the light *away from* a focal point.

A more convenient alternative is the Fresnel ("fray-NEL") lens. Developed in the 1800s by a French physicist and engineer, the Fresnel lens was originally designed for use in lighthouses, increasing the luminosity of common lighthouse lamps of the time by a factor of four. In the Cordouan lighthouse in 1823, the lens allowed light to be seen twenty miles away. Fresnel lenses are compact, and their concentric rings allow them to capture light from more oblique sources. They range in size from eight by eleven inches to the size of a credit card. Bigger is better because, like a parabolic dish, a bigger lens captures and focuses more light, but ones the size of a credit card will work for your survival kit. More important than the size is the magnification. I recommend trying to find one that offers at least 4–5x magnification.

Other options for lenses that can focus sunlight are detachable camera lenses and, possibly, a rifle scope. Both can often magnify the sun's rays enough to get tinder to catch, but much like the magnifying glass, they require direct sunlight in order to work.

USING WATER AND ICE AS A LENS

WATER IN A GLASS OR PLASTIC BOTTLE

Put a little water in the bottom of a clear container. On a bright day, hold it up to the sun and, if you tilt it just so, the rays will shine through the water like a lens to a focal point. If you position the focal point on tinder, you can often generate enough heat to light it.

Primitive fire teacher Gary Gonzales has demonstrated this tactic and has produced an ember in under two minutes, but it often takes longer. Success with this method requires a clear sky, a clear container (preferably without ridges), and a lot of patience.

ICE

The Inuit, who often hunt in freezing Arctic conditions, have been known to use a huge sheet of ice, about four feet in diameter, to create a lens to start fires. Success with this method requires a clear piece of ice, which you can then carefully scrape to create enough of a lens to focus light onto your tinder. This method takes skill and patience, so it will probably only be used in the rare case when conditions are right and you're in survival mode.

REFLECTING FROM A LENS

THE ALUMINUM CAN

On a clear day with direct sunlight, you can actually make a fire using the bottom of an aluminum can. While not a true parabolic dish, a highly polished surface can be used to focus the sun's rays to a point and ignite tinder. Aluminum cans are discarded everywhere, and this other use makes them extremely valuable "trash." This method can also be accomplished using other curved metallic surfaces, such as a metal salad bowl or a curved plate, if you have them in your pack.

To get the high polish you need to start a fire, the best option is using fine steel wool—or even toothpaste if that's all you have. You'll need to polish the bottom for about fifteen to twenty minutes. Before you begin polishing, use a rag or a cotton T-shirt to wipe off the surface, rubbing and polishing as you do. Then, put the steel wool to work and continue alternating between the two. The fabric will help remove any residue the wool leaves behind and lets you track your progress. You'll have to repeat the process several times, but when you're done, the bottom of the can should be highly reflective, almost mirrorlike. How do you know you're done? The only way to know is to test it.

Aim the bottom of the can toward the sun, watching to see where the light focuses to a point. When you find that point, move your tinder there and hold both the can and your tinder stable until the

Parabolic surfaces like solar cookers can be used to harness the sun's energy for a fire.

tinder starts to smoke. You may need to brace the can or hold your arm on something to hold it steady, as this process can take a while. This is akin to making a fire with a magnifying glass, except that instead of focusing the light through a lens, you're reflecting it to a single point.

Fire researcher Eric Zammit found that he could fairly easily ignite tinder such as rolled mugwort leaves using this method, as long as the bottom of the can was highly polished, and as long as it was close to midday, when the sun was directly overhead. Though he was able to ignite leaves, he could not ignite paper.

FLASH TORCH

Another, more modern, alternative is the military grade FlashTorch Mini. While most headlamps range from 50 to 500 lumens, the

The bamboo fire saw uses two components to produce an ember: the wooden "saw" itself, and a hearth, also called a fireboard.

FlashTorch Mini produces 2,300 lumens. Part of a class of new flash-lights to hit the market, the halogen light in the Mini can light a fire and, as advertised, fry an egg. If you decide this is the method for you but want a different model, be sure to purchase a flashlight with as many lumens as the Mini. Some lights with similar names aren't powerful enough to start a fire.

USING FRICTION AS A FIRE STARTER

Before matches and magnifying glasses, humans relied on the heat caused by friction to light fires and developed a myriad of methods for doing so. Each method has its pros and cons, and we'll explore a few of the most common. All of these methods require a lot of energy and are much more likely to be successful if you've practiced at home.

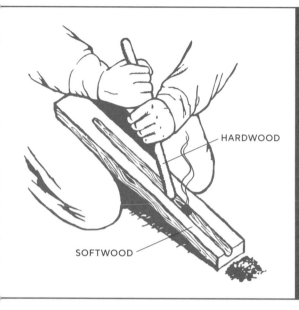

HARDWOOD

SOFTWOOD

The fire plow uses two pieces of wood, rubbing one against the other to produce friction and heat, eventually creating a spark.

THE PLOW

In the movie *Cast Away*, a stranded Tom Hanks figured out how to get a fire going using a method known as the plow, which uses two pieces of wood and, as you'll recall if you've seen the film, a lot of effort and a pretty hearty dose of frustration.

The plow consists of a drill, ideally about two feet long and perhaps three times as thick as a pencil, and a base. The base piece or "hearth" is a larger piece of dry wood, ideally at least a half foot wide and maybe two feet long. The wood you use for this will depend on where you are and what's available, but generally speaking you want to use a softwood that isn't resinous (like pine). Ideally, both the drill and the hearth are made of the same wood. Yucca and cedar are two of the best materials. Others that will work well are aspen, red elm, basswood, walnut, blue beech, cypress, cottonwood, and tamarack.

Once you've found the best wood available to you, secure the hearth with your foot and then, holding the drill with both hands, lean into the hearth with the drill. Holding it firmly, quickly push the drill back and forth, back and forth against the hearth, which quickly creates a groove. Your drill will tend to stay in this groove and, after a ton of rubbing, smoke will appear from the sides and the very tip of the groove. Eventually, if all goes right, dust at the tip of the groove will develop into a red-hot ember, which you can then put into tinder and blow into a flame. If you're wise like Tom Hanks, you'll even place your tinder next to the groove so that the ember doesn't have far to travel before it can catch.

While it is technically possible to produce a flame using the plow, other methods are more promising and more likely to yield the desired results in much less time and with significantly less effort, especially for beginners.

HAND DRILL

One of the most common methods of starting a fire without matches, the hand drill technique can also be one of the trickiest due to the force with which the drill must be spun.

Start with a flat piece of wood that is a half inch thick and at least twice as wide as the diameter of the drill you plan to use. This is called the fireboard. The drill should be a sturdy, smooth stick that is at least one foot long and a half inch in diameter.

Cut a V-shaped notch in the edge of the fireboard using a knife or rock. Place some dry leaves, bark, or other material below the notch to catch any sparks or embers that form. Prepare a nest of

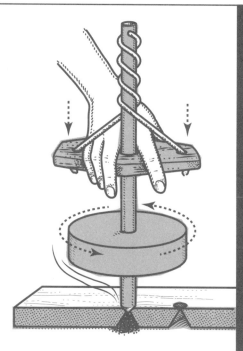

The hand drill is a common method used to start a fire, but must be spun very quickly to create enough friction.

tinder near the fireboard. While sitting or kneeling, hold down the fireboard with your knees, or ask a friend to hold it down for you. Positioning the drill between both your hands, start spinning the drill rapidly by running your hands down it, while simultaneously pressing it down into the notch. Continue running your hands down the drill and quickly moving them back to the top. The faster you spin, and the more pressure you apply against the fireboard, the more friction you will produce, which will cause the fireboard to smoke and create hot dust. Once enough sparks fall into the dry material you have placed below the fireboard, carefully move the material over to the bundle of tinder and gently blow on it to ignite the flame. Continue adding fuel until a fire is formed.

FIRE PISTON

Some of the other fire-starting methods above rely on pressure and repeated movements to create friction and produce heat. The fire piston, however, relies on compression.

There are many variations of the fire piston, but they all have a handle connected to a long dowel, and the dowel fits perfectly into a long hole in a second piece. This tool must be carefully created to get a good fit.

The very tip of the dowel is hollowed out, so you can insert some tinder into it. The dowel should be oiled and kept clean so it slides easily into the hole. The dowel also has a ring on it, comparable to the rings on your car's pistons, to trap the air when you whack the dowel into the hole. (If the ring wears down, you will need to replace it.)

To operate your fire piston, put a little bit of tinder into the tip of the dowel. Holding the dowel in your right hand, place the tip of the dowel carefully into the hole. Then, holding the tool with your left hand, quickly smack the dowel into the hole. This process of forcefully compressing air heats the molecules in a burst of energy. Believe it or not, this simple process can raise the temperature of air inside the cylinder to more than eight hundred degrees Fahrenheit. Then, rapidly pull out the dowel, and if it all went well, you'll have an ember in the tinder that's in the hollow of the dowel.

For this to work well, the dowel must be kept clean and oiled, and you need the ideal tinder. I found that as I used my fire piston,

ISHI'S LESSON

In 1911, an approximately fifty-year-old Yahi Native American man walked out of the forest into the little town of Oroville, near the foothills of Lassen Peak, in Northern California. He had survived in the wild, the last of his tribe, and now he was alone. Anthropologists came to study this living window into the past of the indigenous people of that part of the Americas.

Among other things, he shared his method of making fire, probably the most widely practiced method of friction fire making in history. The details have been recorded by Theodora Kroeber in *Ishi in Two Worlds*.

According to Kroeber, "No manufactured object could be less complicated than Ishi's fire drill, which consists of a lower and an upper piece: a woman piece and a man piece, as he symbolized them. The hearth, or lower piece, is a flat slab of wood which should be somewhat softer than the wood of the shaft or twirler. . . . The drill, or upper piece, is an ordinary round stick of a size to fit the hearth socket, about the length of an arrow shaft, but larger at one end."

Kroeber goes on to describe how Ishi placed various kinds of tinder around the notch in the hearth board and rapidly spun the drill between his hands, eventually creating an ember.

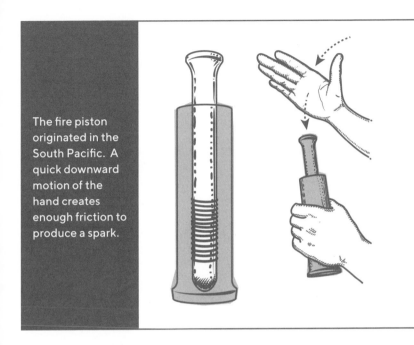

The fire piston originated in the South Pacific. A quick downward motion of the hand creates enough friction to produce a spark.

it became dirty and didn't work quickly. I ended up storing it in a separate container in order to keep it clean and functioning well, but it still wore out. So, while the fire piston required much less energy, could be used with one hand, and was often more effective than some of the other methods (at least for beginners), because it cannot be readily fabricated in the woods in an emergency, it's not one of my top choices for making a fire.

FLINT AND STEEL

Flint and steel preceded matches as one of the earliest forms of fire making and remain one of the most widely practiced methods throughout the world. Unlike the plow, the flint and steel method is much more resistant to moisture, cold temperatures, and strong winds. Using a flint and steel creates sparks by the friction of the two different materials striking each other. For this method you'll need flint, steel, tinder to catch the spark, and kindling laid out to catch the tinder once you've got it going.

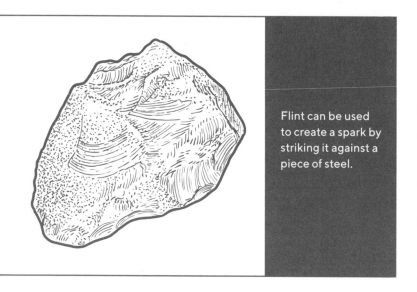

Flint can be used to create a spark by striking it against a piece of steel.

Flint is a sedimentary rock, often chert, which creates a spark when you strike it against hardened steel. When it comes to finding chert, anywhere that was once an ocean will have some available, hence its availability in the southeast and midwest parts of the United States. In the Northeast, quartzite is a metamorphic rock that can be used like flint to start fires, and agate is an available source in the Midwest. A beach cobble is also an option. If you break it open and its

HOW DOES IT WORK?

Striking a steel against the edge of a sharp rock creates a steel shaving. The force of the friction makes the shaving ignite.

insides reveal a sparkling texture, that means a high quartz content, which works well for fire making.

If you choose to scavenge for flint rather than purchase a flint and steel kit, you'll want to start near riverbeds. Because chert is so hard, other stones will erode away in the water, often leaving a pile of chert pebbles along the banks.

You also need a piece of high-carbon steel. My very first steel was from a Girl Scout fire-making kit. It was just a flat piece of an old carbon steel file. You can also purchase what are called bastard files from the hardware store and use them with great success. (That being said, if you plan to use a thrift-store find or hand-me-down file, be sure to practice at home.) Any steel that you use to successfully create an ember will have a high carbon content. Some steel won't work to start a fire. There are numerous options online for purchasing a flint and steel kit, and any outdoor store worth its weight will carry some as well. If you're drawn to the tradition and art of the craft, some blacksmiths still make the C-shaped steels used expressly for fire making.

Gather some tinder together. Willow or cattail fluff will ignite well with a spark, but most flint and steel practitioners prefer to use something called charcloth for their tinder. (See sidebar on making charcloth.)

First, practice striking the flint with your steel so you can feel the amount of strength and pressure required to produce a shower of sparks. Here's a good method for a right-handed person:

Hold the steel striker in your right hand, and hold a flake of flint in your left hand, between your thumb and index finger. To produce sparks, strike down hard onto the flint with the striker and follow through. It should be a sharp, perpendicular edge-to-edge strike.

Then, place a bit of charcloth (or other tinder) either directly under the flint or between your next two fingers. Now strike again, and watch the black charcloth. If you produced a good shower of sparks, one of them might stick on the charcloth. Sometimes you don't see it at first, but a small spot on the charcloth will be glowing red. If so, you've captured a spark.

Now gently blow onto the charcloth, and watch the ember grow. Quickly place the charcloth into your prepared kindling. Gently blow into the bundle or place it in a breeze. The ember will grow. Continue doing this until your kindling bursts into flame.

CHEMICAL FIRE STARTERS

FLARE

Do you carry a flare in your car for signaling to other drivers in a roadside emergency? The chemical in one of these flares makes an excellent fire starter. You typically peel off the top and scrape the two

MAKING CHARCLOTH

Charcloth is a terrific man-made tinder. It is commonly created from old cotton pants or T-shirts and a small metal container, such as a shoe-polish tin, that has a snug-fitting lid.

Cut up pieces of the cotton so they all fit neatly into the tin. Punch a nail-sized hole into the lid of the tin, and put the lid on securely. Now place the tin into a fire. White smoke should puff out of the hole in a few minutes. After five minutes or so, knock the tin out of the fire and let it cool. When you open the lid, you should have all black charcloth.

If the cotton is obviously only partially charred, put the lid back on the tin and place it back into the fire for a few more minutes.

If you opened up the tin and everything inside is all white ash, that means your little hole was too big, and you just burned the cotton to ash, which means you have to try again.

If you end up with what looks like a little hockey puck, that means you had polyester instead of cotton. Throw it away and start all over with 100% cotton.

pieces together to get an ignition. The flare will then burn hotly for fifteen to thirty minutes, and you can use this to light tinder. If your car won't start and you have to spend the night in the winter woods, use the flare to get that fire going!

FERROCERIUM

These days, every backpacking and camping store has dozens of clever new ways to make a fire. Most are based on a ferrocerium (or "ferro") rod, which is a black rod about the thickness of a pencil (they vary) and anywhere from a few inches to half a foot long. While they're widely available, not all ferro rods are made equal, and cheaper versions may not function very well. Softer ferro rods may produce sparks more easily, but the sparks won't be quite as hot. Harder ferro rods may take more practice or a sharper edge to create a spark, but the sparks they do produce will burn hotter.

Once you've purchased a quality rod, practice to ensure you have the proper technique. You'll need to scrape the rod with something (referred to as a scraper or striker) to initiate the spark. While a knife is an option, repeated use can wear down the blade. Many rods come with a sharpened scraper, but sharp rocks will also work.

With your scraper in hand, set the end of the ferrocerium rod against (or amid) the tinder you've prepared. Hold the scraper against the rod at a 45-degree angle. Then, rather than moving the scraper, pull the road back against it to create a spark or, better yet, a shower of sparks.

Ferro rods won't last forever. Depending on the quality of the rod and the frequency of use, these rods may last anywhere from a month to a couple of years.

MAGNESIUM FIRE STARTER

A favorite magnesium fire starter is manufactured by Doan, of South Euclid, Ohio. It is a little rectangle made of magnesium and other ingredients—the mix is kept secret by the manufacturer—and a thin ferrocerium rod secured to the long end of the rectangle.

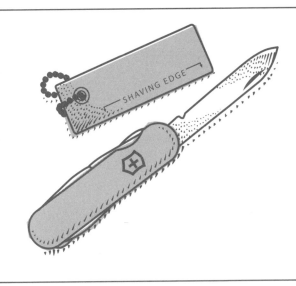

Use your pocketknife to scrape off shavings from the magnesium fire starter onto a pile of tinder.

SHAVING EDGE

This magnesium fire starter measures about an inch wide by three inches long and is about a quarter inch thick, with a hole drilled into the rectangular bar so that it can be carried at all times on a key chain. What makes it the best out of the myriad fire-starter tools currently available is its simplicity—there are no moving parts (so there's nothing to break) and nothing to refill (so no liquids are necessary). Also, while there is a variety of knock-off Doan's-style starters, I have found that most do not work as well as the original.

To use it, you take your knife and scrape a pile of magnesium onto some tinder and then you scrape the built-in ferrocerium rod to produce a shower of sparks. If you have difficulty with a magnesium fire starter, make sure you get a sufficient pile of shavings, and remember to stay out of the wind, where the pile can easily blow away. If your knife is dull, or you're not bearing down hard enough, you'll end up with a little pile of small shavings. Try again.

USING A ROUND OF SHOTGUN AMMO

If you're out hunting, and you get lost and need to spend the night in the woods, there is a way to make a fire with your shotgun and some ammo.

You can carefully cut open the top of a shotgun round, remove the wadding, and pour the powder into tinder. If the sun is still high in the sky, you can use your rifle scope lens to light the tinder. Otherwise, you'll have to rely on one of the other fire-starting methods we've outlined above. Whatever method you use to get the fire started, be sure you have good tinder and kindling set up to receive it. The powder will light and provide good flame for a moment, but it will extinguish quickly.

If it happens to be nighttime or an overcast day, there's another way to make a fire with your shotgun. Using extreme caution, cut open the top of the shotgun round and remove the wadding. Insert some cotton into the round, such as a piece of cotton you've cut from your handkerchief or clothing. (Make sure it's cotton, not polyester, which won't burn as well.) Close the top of the round, if you can. Load the round, and fire it in a safe direction. It won't go very far, as it's just cotton. But the fabric will come out burning, or glowing, and you should put it quickly into your carefully prepared tinder.

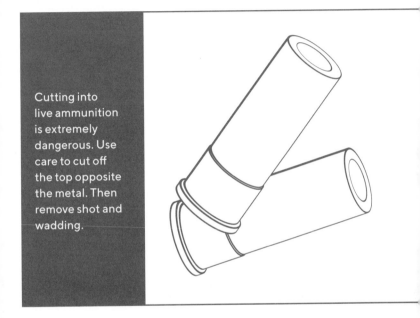

Cutting into live ammunition is extremely dangerous. Use care to cut off the top opposite the metal. Then remove shot and wadding.

ELECTRIC FIRE STARTERS

The ever-present cell phone that we cart around as a GPS device or camera can also provide for us when it comes to starting a fire. In fact, anything that uses a battery—think headlamps or GPS units— can help you make fire. Let's look at some of the ways in which you can tap electricity for the purpose of making your campfire.

MAKING FIRE FROM A CAR BATTERY

Let's say your car breaks down in the woods. You didn't bring any emergency gear because you were just going to dinner, and you didn't expect to spend the night in the middle of the forest. What now?

The easiest way to make a fire from your car is with your cigarette lighter. First, collect your flammable tinder and prepare your fire ring in a safe place. Push in your cigarette lighter and, once it pops out red hot, press some tinder into the hot end. Blow on it gently until you get your flame. Then add it to the tinder in your fire ring.

66 Anything that uses a battery—headlamps or GPS units—can help you make fire. **99**

But many cars no longer have cigarette lighters. Now what? Pop the hood of your vehicle and locate your battery, which is that black rectangular object, typically with two fat wires coming out of it, one of which is usually black and the other red.

Next, find your jumper cables, which you should always include as part of your car's emergency gear. Carefully attach the jumper cables to the terminals at the end of each battery, keeping the two free ends from touching, with the red (positive) end going to the red spot on the battery and the black (negative) end aligning with the black.

Although you *could* randomly strike the two free terminals of your jumper cables and get a spark, that's not a safe way to do it. Instead, using the teeth of the clamp on a free end of your jumper cables, grasp a paper clip or a small piece of wire. Wrap it with a bit of flammable tinder, such as cotton or mugwort or other dry leaves. Then, carefully touch the remaining free clamp to the wire, and the tinder should ignite as electricity flows through the wire.

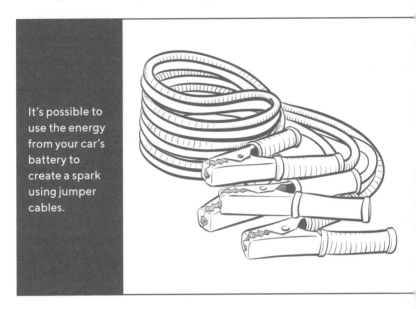

It's possible to use the energy from your car's battery to create a spark using jumper cables.

Be ready to add that little flame to your prepared pile of tinder and make your fire. As you do that, be careful to secure the jumper cables so the two free ends do not touch, which could cause a spark—or even explode your battery. Quickly remove the jumper cables from your battery.

NO JUMPER CABLES?

Oh no! You don't have jumper cables in your car? You should still be able to coax a fire from your car battery, though it might be a bit harder.

The key is to make a bridge between the positive and the negative terminals of the battery. One of the best ways to do this is with a piece of fine steel wool. Assuming you have some steel wool in your car, you take a piece about a foot long. Touch one end to one battery terminal and touch the other end of the steel wool to the other terminal, and watch out! The steel wool will quickly start to burn. Get it out of the engine compartment quickly and onto some prepared tinder, carefully blowing it to a flame.

Another option is to use a short piece of fine wire, no thicker than a paper clip. It has to be long enough to reach from one battery terminal to the other. Connect the terminals with the wire, and it should quickly start to get hot. Be ready to wrap some dry cotton or other fibrous material around the wire, which should catch fire fairly quickly.

MAKING A FIRE FROM FLASHLIGHT BATTERIES

D, C, AA, AAA, and 9-volt batteries can all be used to make a fire, though using the 9-volt is the easiest. Simply press the terminals of the 9-volt battery onto some fine steel wool and—presto!—the steel wool begins to burn. With the other batteries, you need to stretch the steel wool from the top terminal to the bottom terminal. Don't hold the steel wool against a terminal, but rather, touch it lightly

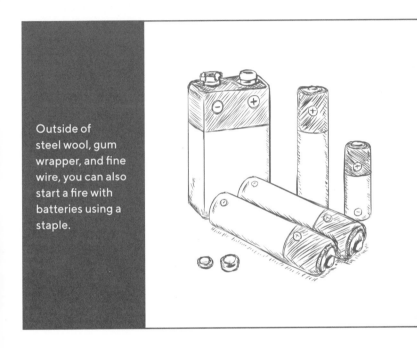

Outside of steel wool, gum wrapper, and fine wire, you can also start a fire with batteries using a staple.

and move it about until you see the spark begin. If your batteries are not at a full charge (or if you're using lower-voltage batteries such as AAs or AAAs), you can try stacking at least two of them, and starting over.

You can also use wires or foil gum wrappers to light a fire using a battery.

Unlike the steel wool, you'll want to hold each end of the gum wrapper or wire tight to the opposing terminals of the battery. Wear gloves, in case your materials get hot.

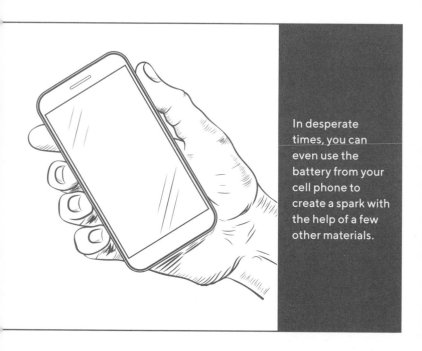

In desperate times, you can even use the battery from your cell phone to create a spark with the help of a few other materials.

With the wire method, ensure a coil of wire is resting on your tinder. Shape the gum wrapper like a piece of bow-tie pasta so that it's thinnest in the middle, which will help it to heat faster. Much like the wire method, you want this thin part of the bow tie to be resting on the tinder. This may be difficult (depending on the size of your battery) as the gum wrapper is much smaller. If the wrapper can't rest directly on the tinder, be sure to have the tinder nearby so you can transport the wrapper (your heat source) to the tinder quickly.

OTHER BATTERIES

These days, most people have batteries in their electronic devices, such as cell phones or cameras. However, taking them out will often ruin the phone, so this should be done only in extreme situations. For a cell phone, you will need to power the phone off and remove the back, usually through the USB port. (However, some phones have screws.) Once the back is off, the phone's flat square battery is relatively easy to remove. When you look at the terminals, you'll see three contact points. The easiest way to create a fire from this battery is with the finest steel wool or with aluminum foil. Simply press the steel wool onto the outer terminals, and in a few seconds the steel wool or foil will be sparking. You can use that to light your tinder.

4

Fuel

—— ✕ ——

From Ember to Flames

> *"There is always enchantment in the closing hour when the fading coals in the fire stir and 'speak' their soft good night."*
>
> Conrad Meinecke

Whether you simply struck a match or spent a great deal of energy ushering embers forth with friction, you've got the beginnings of a fire and accomplished what is likely the most challenging part of starting a fire. But your work isn't over. The next step is nurturing those initial flames into something bigger.

GETTING YOUR FLAME TO GROW

Depending on the tinder you use and the conditions outside, keeping the ember alight might mean blowing on it gently, feeding it more fuel, or protecting it from the wind. And the process of moving from ember to full-blown fire starts at the kind of tinder you've prepared.

STAGE ONE:

Begin with fine, fluffy tinder that holds together well. Dry grass or wood shavings are easy to form into a bird's nest shape (the perfect bed for your tinder) and hold together nicely. Your bird's nest bundle needs to be light and airy, but it cannot have so many air pockets that you simply lose your ember as it breaks into smaller pieces. This is why a bundle of pine needles doesn't often work. You want material that cradles the ember while allowing oxygen to pass through and fan it into flames.

Carefully place your ember into your fluffy tinder bundle, and then gently breathe on it. Careful! If you blow too hard you run the risk of extinguishing the ember or scattering it into tiny pieces on the ground, where it will self-extinguish. Begin gently puffing and increase the strength of your breaths when you see that the ember is growing.

STAGE TWO:

Next, wrap your initial bird's nest bundle with a slightly bigger bundle consisting of material like dry grass, pine needles, shredded bark, or newspaper.

Now you can hold your growing bundle much more easily, and you can blow into it with a bit more force. If all is going well, your tinder bundle will be producing increasingly more smoke, and the ember will have grown and spread through the tinder. You can start blowing a bit harder. Don't hold your face too close to the bundle or you might burn your eyelashes. If it's a windy day, you can often just hold the tinder in the wind. Very soon, it will burst into flame. Place your burning bundle into your fire ring.

STAGE THREE:

Now add kindling, the next level of burnable materials. Kindling should consist of wood the thickness of pencils, dry bark, leaves, and perhaps some pine needles to generate more heat. Indoors it can mean dry cardboard, newspaper, or homemade fire starters (like those described in the fire starter section).

You don't want to smother your new fire, so add kindling slowly, ensuring a constant flow of air through the fire so that you don't put it out.

THE FIRE LAY

Once you've got a good flame and have kindling to it, you'll want to build your fledgling fire into something more substantial. Below are the most common fire lays, which can be used both indoors and out and will work in a variety of conditions, some better than others. With all fire lays, be sure to leave gaps between kindling and logs when you stack them, to allow for the airflow that feeds the fire.

TIPI (OR TEPEE)

One option is the simple tipi fire lay. Place straight sticks over your little fire, so that they all come to a point in the middle, like a tipi. Sometimes, a stout vertical stick is pushed into the middle of your fire-to-be to provide support, and then the other twigs are leaned onto this central stake. Leave an opening on the side where any breeze is

Fires structures in a tipi style are easy to light, fast to flame, and quickly fall into a neat pile of coals.

blowing, so the flames get the air they need and the wind pushes the flames into the kindling. As the flame licks up and starts to burn the tipi, you can add more sticks as needed. When the structure falls over, you can add fuel logs on top.

LOG CABIN

Remember Lincoln Logs? Little did you know when you mastered the art of tiny cabin building that you were training for one of the tried-and-true fire lay methods. This "log cabin" method is a lot like playing with Lincoln Logs. Start by placing larger twigs around one to three inches from the flame (depending on the length of kindling you have), around the base of your fire in a square. Next, place a layer of kindling across the square, and on top of that, another (alternating so that the kindling in every other layer runs perpendicular to the kindling layers above and below). It's easiest if you do two opposite ends first, and then lay on the next perpendicular pair. Just keep

THE "MIRACLE" FIRE STARTER

Harvest some "fatwood" from dead pine tree stumps if conditions are right (or if you have the chance to purchase it before you're building your campfire). This old, dead wood from the core of the tree or the joints where it was connected to limbs becomes saturated with resin as the roots and bark rot away, and knots of dense, highly flammable wood remain. If you're purchasing it online, it will come already split into small sticks that you can shave or light as is. If you forage for your own, you'll want to shave or trim off smaller pieces, as a little goes a long way.

stacking, which helps to define your fire and gives your little flame something more to burn. As your cabin burns, you make another bigger one around it. Eventually, you'll have a good bed of coals, and you can just add logs.

LEAN-TO

The lean-to fire lay begins with a low tripod of twigs, where two are short and one twig is longer. Then add more twigs and pine needles over the lean-to. The lean-to shape gives the new flame some oxygen, and the new twigs won't smother the flame. There are many variations of the lean-to lay, one being simply leaning twigs from the edge of your stone fire circle, extended so that they are just above the little flame.

Constructing your fire as a lean-to is a great way to ensure your flame gets plenty of oxygen, helping it grow.

HAYSTACK

The haystack looks like it sounds, and it's built by simply laying small dry tinder around and over your little flame every which way. But while the haystack may look less organized than the other fire lays, it still requires care to ensure that you don't compress too much material at once and smother your flame. If everything is wet or even just damp, this method isn't the best because wet conditions require a bit more care to get a good fire going. But under dry conditions, the simple haystack should work fine for getting your fire going well. As you build your kindling up, you'll create a bed for larger fuels. Keep laying fuel down in every direction as needed, leaving enough room for airflow.

STAGE FOUR:

TIME FOR LOGS!

When it comes to selecting the best wood, a basic understanding of the anatomy of a log can be helpful. While the specifics vary from one tree species to the next, most trees have some version of the following. On the outermost layer, trees are covered with bark. Bark is replaced consistently and is sort of like a shell for the tree, keeping moisture out during rain and keeping it in during drought. Bark keeps the tree warm and acts as a barrier against insect infestation. Underneath the bark is the cambium. This cell layer is constantly growing, producing new bark and new sapwood, which is the layer beneath it. As the cambium grows more and more layers of sapwood, the innermost layers die and become part of the central core of the tree, called heartwood. This pillar is strong as steel, bound together by cellulose fibers and a unique chemical called lignin.

WOOD SELECTION

Fuel wood is logs that will burn for an extended period of time. In general, choosing the best wood comes down to what kind of wood is available and choosing wood that has a high British Thermal Unit, or BTU, rating. BTUs are a measure of the amount of heat energy available in any given substance. The more BTUs, the hotter or longer your fire will burn.

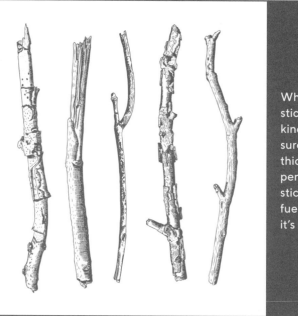

When gathering sticks to use as kindling, make sure they are no thicker than a pencil. Save larger sticks and logs to fuel the fire once it's burning well.

In terms of ideal wood selection, hardwoods are best, for both indoor and outdoor fires. Common hardwoods are oak, ash, and maple, which take longer to catch fire but burn for a long time. Softwoods like pine and cedar are best avoided indoors, except perhaps when starting the fire. Their oil content causes them to burn very hot and often crack and pop erratically as hot embers fly about. Look at Appendix 2 for the relative BTU content of different trees in North America.

When camping, use only local firewood. Do not bring wood from more than fifty miles away, as you may be introducing foreign insects into the forest. If you are gathering wood in the forest, collect downed pieces that break easily, as it is more likely to be dry. Use gloves and look away when snapping a branch to protect your eyes. If it bends, the wood is probably too wet or green to burn efficiently, at least in the early stages of your fire. If you do need to use it, remove the outer bark and the thin layer beneath the bark to increase your chances of success.

LOW-COST OPTIONS FOR HOME USE

Tree pruners and arborists cut down trees constantly, and they need to dispose of that wood. Sometimes, they have an arrangement with a wood lot that will trim it to size and sell it back to the consumer. One of your best choices for getting free or low-cost firewood is to locate the arborists in your area and arrange to pick up some of their wood or have it delivered. You may have to rush to a tree-pruning site on short notice in order to take advantage of their available wood.

In addition to contacting local arborists, our public lands, managed by the Bureau of Land Management (BLM) and the US Forest Service, provide opportunities for you to collect wood for home or personal use. For small amounts, you might not even need a permit on BLM land. On most Forest Service lands, firewood permits cost around $20 and allow you to collect up to four hundred cubic feet (the equivalent of nearly four full-size truck beds). Check your local regulations and visit BLM or Forest Service offices to get a permit, a map

While hardwoods take longer to catch than other logs, common types such as oak, ash, and maple all burn for a long time once the fire is underway.

of designated areas where cutting trees is allowed, and any specific restrictions or requirements.

BUYING YOUR FIREWOOD

If you plan to purchase your wood, here are a few tips that utilize all of your senses for ensuring the wood has been properly seasoned before you truck it home:

- Perform a "radial check." There should be cracks in the end grains of the wood.

SEASON FOR A SEASON

As you've read throughout the book, using dry wood is important for the success of your fire, and it's a safety consideration too. Wood with a higher moisture content produces more creosote and smoke, which can clog your chimney and stress your lungs. As a general rule, firewood that you collect from an arborist or that you harvest, split, and stack yourself should dry for at least a season before burning. More specifically, it should have a moisture content of no more than 20 percent, which you can check using a moisture meter. These meters run the gamut in cost and effectiveness, but for the purpose of checking firewood, you can get a decent one for around $40.

- Wood fades and darkens as it seasons, so stay away from stacks of freshly cut, bright wood (unless you plan to season it yourself).

- Smell and feel the wood. If it's moist or cool to the touch, it likely has a moisture content of over 20 percent. If it smells sappy, it's likely too freshly cut.

- Look at the bark—it should be peeling back on its own. If you plan to purchase a cord of wood, most of it should have already lost its bark.

- Seasoned wood should feel light and, if you bang two pieces together, sound hollow.

Firewood available for purchase is often measured in cords, and a standard cord is 128 cubic feet of wood, or a stack of wood that's 4' deep × 4' tall × 8' long. Most vendors will sell in full, half, and quarter cords, though you'll get the best deal when purchasing a full cord. And while exactly how much wood you use will depend on how cold it is, how large your home is, how often you're heating your home, and what other heating sources you use, homeowners who heat primarily with wood will, as a rule of thumb, burn about five cords throughout a winter.

SPLITTING LOGS

Whether you've collected all your wood from nearby public lands or purchased a cord from a local dealer, you're likely to be splitting logs. In the case of wood you've collected yourself, the task at hand is a much larger undertaking. But even if you purchase ready-to-burn wood, you may want to chop it into small pieces for kindling. Splitting green wood is possible, and the wood will dry out better when split. But you will learn that most woods split a lot better after they are seasoned.

Much like starting a fire properly, splitting wood is much, much easier (and safer) if you have the proper tools. You need sturdy gloves, several wedges, and a splitting maul, which is like a combination of a sledgehammer and an axe. You don't necessarily need an axe, except perhaps occasionally for smaller logs, as the head often become stuck in the wood with larger logs.

You'll need a flat surface as a base for your logs, also referred to as a chopping block. While you can chop wood directly on the ground, it isn't as safe, and your back, arms, and legs won't appreciate it. Splitting on a block creates further distance between the axe or maul and your feet, decreases the chance of deflecting off of things like rocks, and gives you more power by creating a firm surface so that the bulk of your blow is absorbed by the log you're trying to cut, rather than by the earth beneath it.

When it comes to selecting the proper chopping block, you're essentially looking for exactly the kind of wood you *don't* want to split—knotty wood. A thick, flared stump that's twelve to sixteen inches tall and wider than the wood you plan to split will make for a solid chopping block.

Once you've got your chopping block in place, set a log upright in the center of it. Whack it with your maul. If the wood is dry, you can often split it in two with a good whack. If the wood is green, it's

The best wood for a chopping block is knotty type that is hard to split, such as elm or sugar maple. It should be several inches wider than the wood you are splitting.

heavier with water, which means it sometimes takes more whacks to split.

For hard-to-split larger logs, whack the log with the maul, and then place a wedge into the crack you just created. Then whack the wedge, and maybe even add a second wedge in some cases.

MAUL AND AXE SAFETY

A maul weighs more than an axe and has a head more like a sledge-hammer than a sharpened edge. A maul is usually recommended as a wood-splitting tool over an axe, since they both serve the same function, but the risks of a missed swing are higher with an axe than with a maul, given the sharp blade. However, some people prefer the lighter weight of an axe, which can make it easier to wield. If you're accident prone, it might be best to opt for a maul to start. Buy a maul that suits your body size and your ability. A six-pound maul is a good starting place, as it's heavy enough to split most wood but won't tire you out. In addition to a maul, invest in at least one driving wedge— or several of various sizes.

If you're new at this, begin by hoisting the maul over your shoul-der (your right shoulder, assuming you are right-handed) and then just swing it down onto the upended log. Didn't split the log? No worries, you'll get better with practice.

When using either an axe or a maul, start first by clearing the area around you. Be sure to remove any brush or branches that are within axe- or maul-length. Remove any tripping hazards.

To properly hold an axe if you're right-handed, let your left hand sit just above the knob at the end of the handle with your palm facing toward you. With your right hand, grasp the axe just below the head. The way you swing will depend on what you're trying to do—felling a tree vs. splitting wood. But regardless of the task at hand, it's important to focus on accuracy rather than power.

The axe is one of humanity's oldest and most versatile tools. When it comes to buying the right axe for you, the first thing is to decide whether you'll buy a brand-new or an antique axe. The former has

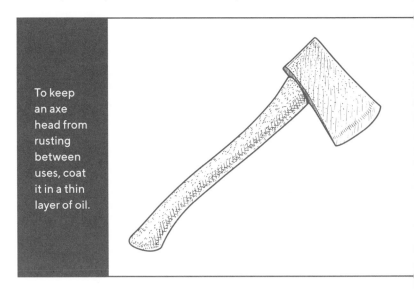

To keep an axe head from rusting between uses, coat it in a thin layer of oil.

obvious benefits insofar as it'll be ready to use immediately. That being said, older axes can be cheaper (and old handles can always be repaired). Next, you'll have to decide if you're after a single- or double-bit axe. While weight is a consideration, double-bit axes also offer the benefit of added control because both ends of the head are of equal weight and length. This kind of balance means less wobble, and less wobble means more safety.

Choosing the right axe will depend both on your planned purpose and your size. Larger axes (heavier with longer handles) may offer more power but less precision. A twenty-eight-inch, two-pound double-bit axe is a fairly versatile option. Personal preference, body type, and primary utility are all considerations, so it's good to do your research.

STACKING AND STORING YOUR WOOD

If you're using wood for heat or cooking, you have to find a dry place outside to store it, where it can lose moisture so it will burn better. You need to keep an eye on it to make sure it doesn't become infested with bugs or rodents.

Timing and organization both come into play here. If the first frosty night hits at the end of October, you'll want to think about purchasing and stacking your wood early in the month to let it dry for a couple of weeks.

Key things to consider when stacking wood are keeping it dry, keeping it organized, and making it easy enough to pull from. To the first point, you'll need a flat surface and a solid foundation to keep the wood off the ground. This foundation layer prevents moisture from the ground from percolating up through the wood and spreading mold and spores. A foundation can be a rack sold at most lumberyards, plywood, cinder blocks, or pallets. Or you can simply sacrifice a few pieces of wood to establish that first layer.

A rack can also be made quite simply with two-by-fours. Your goal is to have a dedicated space to store wood so that it is off the ground, where wood can be stored up to five feet high. If you build your own rack, the base can be two-by-fours set on end for the length of the rack, with shorter two-by-fours cut for the depth of the rack.

" Key things to consider when stacking wood are keeping it dry, keeping it organized, and making it easy enough to pull from. "

Each end of the rack consists of well-secured two-by-fours as high as you want to stack the wood. A few two-by-fours should also be screwed in to define a top area. This gives your wood rack stability, and it allows you to throw a cover over your woodpile in the event of rain.

Ideal drying conditions include exposure to the sun and air movement through the stack. There are many different approaches to wood stacking. Whole books have been written about the subject, in fact. See the sidebar on page 80 for some options.

ALTERNATIVES TO WOOD

While there's a certain inarguable romance about burning wood, this long-heralded fuel type has its downsides. And, particularly for those who are sensitive to smoke or who live where smoke is a problem, these nonwood alternatives mean you get to enjoy all the charm and benefits of fire with fewer of the negatives.

Here are some of the reasons to explore wood alternatives: smoke increases pollution and has negative health effects; burning wood produces carbon monoxide; when burned, wood can leave creosote as a by-product and lead to unwanted (usually chimney) fires; wood can be expensive; and harvesting wood means cutting down trees unnecessarily, given the alternatives listed below.

NONWOOD MATERIALS

Soy-and-switchgrass logs can be used in wood-burning stoves, fireplaces, firepits, and campfires. Made of more than 50 percent soy wax that's pressed together with switchgrass, these logs are slow burning and clean, leaving almost no residue behind. Java-Logs, made of recycled coffee grounds, burn for up to four hours and produce significantly less carbon monoxide and creosote than wood. Wax logs are another alternative, but be sure to purchase those that are not petroleum based (as they come with their own suite of environmental and health concerns). Look instead for wax logs that are plant based.

SAWDUST AND WOOD CHIPS

Wood bricks (aka biomass bricks) are a clean-burning alternative to wood. They're made from recycled sawdust and wood chips. Because they are kiln dried and formed into bricks, they take up less space and burn both hotter and cleaner. And because they're made of natural materials, they are considered safe for cooking. A similar alternative to wood bricks is wood pellets, which are also made from sawdust and lumber mill scraps. Unlike wood bricks, however, pellets require specialty equipment (like a pellet stove, as opposed to a traditional woodstove) or an insert for a patio fireplace or firepit.

5

Different Outdoor Fires for Different Needs

✕

Cooking, Signaling,
and Staying Dry

"The echoes of beauty you've seen transpire,
resound through dying coals of a campfire."

Ernest Hemingway

What you do after your fire is burning largely depends on your circumstances and whether you're building a fire to stay warm, to cook, to dry your clothes, to gather around, to signal, to stay hidden, or some combination of these.

COOKING

When you start your fire with cooking in mind, one of the goals should be to produce hot coals, all at the same time. By using wood pieces of the same size, distributed evenly over the kindling, this is possible.

The kind of fire you'll need to prepare your meal depends, in large part, on where you are, what materials you have available, and what's for dinner. If you're out camping near an alpine lake and you just hooked a trout for dinner, for example, a small fire with hot, hot coals will do the trick.

So far, you've learned to get a fire going in your fire ring. For cooking, it can be beneficial to place the rocks for the walls of the fire ring in the shape of a keyhole, with one end circular and the other a rectangle or square. The circular end is used to start the fire and keep the fire going, and the rectangular side provides a space to set up your cooking station away from the flames. Once it's blazing, scoot the fire to the circular end of the ring. Then, carefully push some of the hottest coals from the fire back to the rectangular end of the ring. Now carefully place two or three new rocks into this nest of coals. These rocks become your cooking surface. If you're car-camping or have a small grate, place it across the rocks for your insta-grill. If not, consider the rotisserie option of spearing your fish and placing either end of the "spear" on the rocks you just placed. Continue feeding the main fire while your food cooks and harvesting coals as needed to urge your meal along.

If you're trying to cook in a pot over the fire, a similar method can be used, but you'll want to find flat rocks so that the pot is closer to the coals.

The fire ring you build will dictate the size of your cooking space, so plan ahead when you can. That being said, smaller fires require minimal labor in terms of collecting fuel, and are easy to put out when you're done. Plus, they're safer and more easily managed than larger fires. Especially in the summer, when you don't need the extra heat of the campfire, a little fire is the way to go.

HOBO PACKS

Often referred to as hobo packs, little packets of aluminum foil can make for easy and delicious campfire cooking. One of my favorites is the Cajun broil: wrap chunks of potatoes, sausage (andouille), corn, onions, and garlic in a square of foil. Sprinkle with Cajun seasoning. Fold the edges and crease them tightly. Place your little dinner packet in the coals, propped up against the rocks of your fire ring. Rotate occasionally and test after twenty minutes or so.

Larger fires can come in handy for cooking, but even then they need to be managed appropriately. The flame itself isn't what cooks your food—it's the coals produced in the process that provide a hot-enough source. So it isn't so much the size of your fire as its ability to produce piping hot coals. If you're building a fire specifically for cooking food and have a grate (highly recommended), consider building your fire ring in the shape of a horseshoe. At the head, or closed end, build the rock walls higher and then taper them down toward the ends. Place a larger rock at the head of the fireplace so that it can act as a chimney, guiding the smoke away. This structure, with a grate on top, will allow for high-, medium-, and low-heat cooking, based on the food's proximity to the coals. Once everything has burned down to white-hot coals, you can push the coals around to distribute them under the high, medium and low areas of your fire ring. Place your grate or grill on the fire and prepare your meal. Afterward, be careful to remove the grate and set it out of the way of others (especially children and dogs) while you coax your fire back to life for evening warmth and dessert.

One of the oldest, most creative, and most delicious methods of cooking with fire is to build a pit. This method comes in handy if you're cooking a whole animal but can be used to prepare almost any meal. This takes time and effort, so it should only be used in certain circumstances.

The size of the pit you dig for this style of cooking will be determined by the menu you've prepared. As a rule of thumb, prepare a hole that's approximately one foot wider in every direction than whatever you plan to place in the hole. For now, let's say you're feeding everyone you know and cooking a pig. The hole you prepare might be six feet by four feet, and approximately three feet deep. You'll want to line the pit with stones or bricks to stabilize it and hold the heat.

Cooking fires can be set up in a way that makes it easier for you to prepare a meal over an open flame.

The type of stone you use is important—avoid stones that were ever submerged in water. Bricks are the safest bet.

Now it's time to build your fire. In the case of a pig, it will take the better part of a day to build up enough coals (to a depth of approximately one foot). Build the fire as you normally would and continue feeding it until the right amount of coals has built up.

Season and prepare whatever you plan to cook in the meantime and wrap it with many layers of foil and then wet burlap. You'll want to cap it off by wrapping the thing in heavy wire that both holds it together and can be used as a handle for turning it over (you'll need gloves or the appropriate tools for this). Lower your fare into the pit and quickly cover it up with a metal lid, whatever you can use to keep air from getting into the pit. The cooking time will vary but, for something like a pig, can be up to twelve hours.

DAKOTA PIT

The Dakota pit is another option for a cooking fire. You dig a hole into the ground, a foot or so deep, and then dig a tunnel, which helps feed oxygen to the fire. Build your fire in the hole and place your pot over it, which is an efficient way to cook and use minimal fuel.

If the soil is not too hard, this can be easy and quick to build. You should try it at least once and see if you like it. Where the soil is hard packed, this method is a bit impractical.

BUILDING A SHELTER FIRE RING

If you want to keep warm, it's imperative that you don't build a fire ring close to a primitive shelter. A lean-to or a small brush shelter is all tinder! If you need to heat a primitive shelter, a better way to do this is with rocks. First, build a fire away from the shelter. Then collect the right rocks. You'll want two types of rocks: heating (or pit) stones and a lid stone.

" If you need to heat a primitive shelter, there's no better way than to do it with rocks. "

For heating stones, try to find rocks that are dry. Don't use any that have been submerged in a creek or lake. Once exposed to the heat of the fire, saturated rocks can expand and explode. Choose pit stones that will fit in the pit and are large enough (larger than your fist) to hold heat for a while.

Now look for a flat rock. This will be your lid stone, which goes on top of your other rocks. The lid stone will serve dual functions: holding the heat in longer and minimizing your risk of coming into contact with the hot rocks.

Before placing your heating rocks in the fire, you'll want to prepare a small pit just inside the entry of your shelter. Much like choosing where you place a fire ring, you'll want select the right spot for your small pit: make sure the hot rocks aren't lying on duff or other tinder.

Place the pit stones in your fire and wait an hour or so until they are very hot. Using gloves or tools, roll one or more of the stones into the pit. Place the lid stone on top and enjoy the amazing amount of heat they'll provide for several hours.

If you're in a survival situation, this method might save your life.

SIGNALING FIRES

Fires are a great option for signaling if you're lost. Ancient cultures used fires, typically placed strategically on the tops of high peaks, for signaling. For example, in the Anasazi culture of the American Southwest, there is evidence that fires were built at high points and could be seen for twenty miles or more.

In today's world, a fire is simply saying, "I am here." If you are lost or stranded, you want someone to know where you are. Groups or sequences in a variety of ways have long been used as the international distress signal, so three visible fires is the equivalent of SOS, making it more obvious that you are asking for help.

A traditional fire won't necessarily be seen from great distances, but if you can make a lot of smoke, someone might notice. Build your fire in the open so the smoke won't get dispersed by the trees. If a rescue crew is looking for you, and they see your smoke, it's likely you'll have someone coming in the direction of the fire.

A smoky fire needn't be excessively large, and safety should be your first consideration. The area where you build it should be clear of dried grasses and dead undergrowth. It should be in a clearing where there is a chance that the smoke will rise and be seen.

A fire that is burning well with dried material typically produces minimal smoke. So to create visible smoke, add green or punky (partly decayed) material, and more smoke will be produced.

HIDDEN FIRES

If you are in a situation where you don't want to be noticed but need to build a fire, you need to first find a spot where you are somewhat hidden by the natural contours of the land. This might be deep in a narrow canyon or in a gorge where there are many trees on the surface above you. It could be at the base of an overhang or in a naturally sheltered section of a deep but dry riverbed.

Dig a hole and build a small fire. Make sure all your firewood is dry, and make sure your fire is producing flames rather than smoke. Don't use conifer wood (like pine), which snap and crackle. Find the driest twigs and branches and leaves, and make your fire no bigger than absolutely necessary for your cooking or heating needs.

If you have to evacuate in a hurry, you can quickly cover your small fire and be assured that it is safely out.

BUILDING A FIRE IN WET CONDITIONS

Perhaps one of the more frustrating ironies is how much harder it is to build a fire in wet conditions, when you really need one to get warm. But it isn't impossible, and by taking a few extra measures, you should be dry in no time. If the ground is damp or if it's raining even lightly, you'll want to stay away from low-lying kindling and fire configurations. Opt instead for the tipi or lean-to and build it a foot tall. This extra space allows the heat from your tinder to rise through

In wet or snowy conditions, it's helpful to start your fire on a flat platform made out of rocks or logs, with your tinder placed in the center.

the sticks and dry them out before setting them aflame. In addition to building a fire that allows space, you'll want to start your tipi atop a foundation. This isn't a layer that will burn right away but instead creates a barrier between your initial embers and the wet ground. As the heat from a growing fire draws cool, moist air from the ground, it will become especially challenging to keep things going. Laying down some extra bark, twigs, or firewood on which to place your tinder, and eventually, tipi, will create this important distance between flame and wet ground.

Keep some tinder handy to use in case the first round fails. Begin by collecting all the firewood and tinder you can, wet or dry. It's sometimes easiest to gather dry fuel from beneath the protective canopy of living trees, where it has hopefully remained relatively sheltered. Dry material can also be found by using dead branches still on a tree, or layers of dead bark still on a standing tree. If the bark is wet, peel or carve it off. Exposing the dry, inner wood will increase your odds of success.

In wet conditions, pinewood with sap and resin (which I otherwise urge you to avoid because it can send sparks flying) may be important for beating the downpour. The sap is highly flammable and can offer stronger-burning kindling to help dry out the rest.

In a real downpour, a firepit may turn into more of a mud pit. Instead of digging a pit, build a small mound of dirt to stack your fire atop so that you aren't trying to build flame in a growing pool of water.

When it's raining, it's best to make the fire in an area with natural cover, but that's not always possible. Sometimes, there are only specific areas where fire is allowed, so you'll just need to adapt.

You have to create some way to keep the rain from falling directly onto your fire, at least in the early stages. One method is to pound four thick upright sticks or logs at least two feet long into the ground within the firepit area, and then place pieces of bark on the top, which block some of the rain.

Pile up all the wood you've collected nearby, separating the wet from the dry. Next, produce your flame from one of the many methods described in this book and then mother it by adding the tiniest bits of oily pine needles and eucalyptus bark and potato chip bags and pocket lint—whatever might burn easily. The most aromatic leaves are the best because the presence of aroma means there are oils in those leaves, which means they will burn well.

The early stages of making a fire in the rain are the most critical, so you and your group should huddle around, keeping the rain away from the young embers with your bodies and continually adding tiny twigs to the tiny fire.

There is usually plenty of smoke and minimal heat in the early stages of such a fire, because the twigs and branches are drying out.

Sap from pine needles is highly flammable and can be used to help start a fire in wet conditions.

It can take up to an hour to build up enough coals under these circumstances to produce enough heat to start heating water for coffee and soup on the side. It could take even longer, depending on the intensity of the rain.

Just kept adding bigger and bigger twigs and branches, and as the little material dries out and burns, you'll be developing a solid bed of coals. If all proceeds well, you might be able to add small- to large-size logs to your fire in about an hour and a half. Place the larger logs that you gathered near your kindling fire so they can begin drying out in time to add to the fire when you need them.

If the rain continues or comes down heavier, you will need to create some sort of higher roof or covering for your fire. This can be bark or layers of logs stacked tipi-style around the large fire. As they burn, just keep adding more.

6

A Fire Inside

—— ✕ ——

Fireplaces and Woodstoves

"A house with no fireplace is a house without a heart."

Gladys Taber

When you're bringing your fire into your home, you're probably going to be using a built-in fireplace, a free-standing fireplace, or a woodstove. Those are your primary options, though nowadays there are also a number of wood-free alternatives.

FIREPLACE

We've probably all been there—eager to be warm and cozy and faced instead with a smoldering chunk of newspaper that we can't, for the life of us, get to catch fire. Or perhaps even worse, we're pretty certain the fire is burning, only to have it turn into a pile of smoking tinder. Those days are gone if you follow the tricks and recommendations below for starting a fireplace fire and keeping it going strong.

To begin, ensure your fireplace and chimney are properly cleaned. You should have your chimney professionally cleaned by a chimney sweep once a year. The sweep will remove soot and blockages from creosote. Leaving some ash in the fireplace isn't a bad idea, as it offers insulation, but you don't want more than an inch or so. And you need to have the right tools. In addition to a wood poker, shovel, and slate, you'll need your fire starter, kindling, dry wood, and screen nearby.

This next step is probably one of the greatest tricks of the trade and one of the easiest to forget. When the damper is closed, your chimney is filled with cold, heavy air. If you go straight to starting a fire after opening the damper, that cold air essentially suffocates your fire. Instead, you can "prime the flue," which means pushing the cool air up and out by replacing it with warmer air. One way to do this is by simply opening the damper and letting the warm air in the room start to force the cold air out.

To urge the process along, roll up a piece of newspaper into the shape of a stick. Light one end of the newspaper and hold it as far up the chimney as you can, toward the damper. The newspaper won't stay aflame, but keep lighting it and lifting it into the chimney until you can feel the flow of air reverse and go back up the chimney.

Now your flue is primed, and your odds of success are creeping in the right direction.

If you have a grate, place crumpled newspaper or other fire starters beneath it. If you don't have a grate, this tinder can just be placed in the center of the fireplace on the thin layer of ash you left behind.

Next you'll want to go about stacking. While all the methods outlined in the fire lay section will work, the log cabin approach leaves ample room beneath for your tinder and doesn't require movement around the fire (like the tipi can). If you have a grate, begin by stacking the kindling in a log cabin or crisscross fashion on top of the grate. If not, you can set the kindling directly on top of your tinder. Start with your finest fuels and include a few midweight pieces (roughly the width of your wrist) in the mix.

Before you light the fire starter, be sure you have some additional newspaper or tinder beside you, as well as some heavier fuels, like logs or thicker branches.

Now it's time to put those fancy, foot-long matches to use. Light as much of the newspaper or fire starter as you can and keep pushing unburned sections into the flame. Once the kindling starts to burn, you're in business. It's time for a log.

Lighting paper is one way to get a fire started quickly, as it is highly flammable and can by placed alongside tinder.

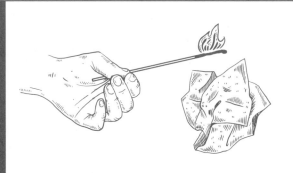

You can continue the crisscross pattern with your logs or shift to the tipi approach. More important than the exact pattern you choose is ensuring that oxygen can continue to circulate around your fuels. If the fire starts dying, you might want to gently blow on it. Or, for a safer and more efficient option, consider using a bellows.

For a fire that can sometimes burn longer and hotter (depending on the conditions and your technique), you can opt for the upside-down approach. To achieve this, simply invert the order of the firewood sizes. Place the largest logs on the bottom of the structure, with increasingly smaller sizes placed atop. The topmost layer should be the kindling and fire starter material. The idea is that, once lit, the smaller fuel will fall to the bottom of the structure, igniting the lower levels and keeping the fire going for a longer duration.

B ellows or "blowing bags" are made in as many forms as there are places in the world that use fire. Pot bellows were used in ancient Egypt, box bellows were used in East Asia, double-piston bellows were used in ancient China as early as the third century BC, and their single-piston relative was developed in the middle of the eighteenth century in Europe. While there are a number of designs and applications, the overarching goal is to increase and target the flow of air, specifically when it comes to blowing on a fire.

Bellows can be cheap (from $10) to hundreds or even thousands of dollars for intricately designed antiques. And, as an added tool in your backcountry kit, you can purchase a handy, lightweight steel bellows that weighs only an ounce.

No matter the fire structure, you'll know when it's time to add more fuel to the fire when there are no longer flames flickering, or when the flames have dwindled to low levels. When placing new fuel, it's important not to suffocate the fire. Without enough oxygen, the fire will put itself out. So, pick a place above any hot coals or flames that doesn't block airflow. Carefully rest the new logs on top of the burning logs at an angle. Blow the coals or flames consistently until the flames roar up again. Then sit back and enjoy the warmth of the rekindled fire.

Now that your fire is going, it's time to put up the screen, restock the pile of logs, get cozy, and watch.

While romantic, nostalgic, and just generally charming, fireplaces are also, unfortunately, notoriously inefficient, with up to 80–90 percent of the heat vanishing up the chimney. The easiest modification to increase the heating quotient of your fireplace is to obtain a grill made from hollow tubes. In theory, when you're burning wood in your fireplace with one of these grills, the cooler air is drawn into the lower part of the tubes, and then hotter air comes out of the top and into your room. Depending on the layout of the room and other factors, most people find a noticeable increase in the ability of the fire to heat the room. Some of these grills have been manufactured with little fans that blow the hot air into your room. These are a significant improvement over the hollow grills alone.

Another way is to modify the chimney. Typically, a fireplace has a single vertical flue, and most of the gases are simply lost to the atmosphere. Sometimes, baffles can be added to slow down the loss of gases and improve the ability of the fireplace to heat your room.

WOODSTOVES

So many woodstoves and in-home fireplaces these days are gas or propane; they flicker on with the flip of a switch. This ease of flame can give the false impression that starting a wood-burning fire in a stove or fireplace should be just as easy, and while it can be, there are definitely ways to make it easier and ways to make it harder. Here are some tricks for a smooth start.

Whether you're working with a fireplace or woodstove, you'll want to start with all valves open. Many woodstoves have a lever by the door or on the back that controls a valve under the grate. This is the best source of oxygen for your fire and a key to your success. The other valve (in a fireplace too) is the damper, which closes the flue, essentially cutting off the flow of air through the chimney.

Next, you'll add your tinder and kindling. Many of the stacking methods mentioned previously will work in a fireplace or woodstove. Light the tinder. If you're working with a woodstove, leave the door open for five minutes or so. Next, add some medium-sized fuels. At this stage, you can close the door most of the way but will want to leave a small crack for another fifteen minutes or so while the fire gets established. Once it's cranking out some heat and most of the fuels are aflame, you can close the door.

After about twenty minutes, and likely the addition of some larger logs and fuels, you'll want to reduce the amount of air going into the stove to slow down the burn rate a bit. Remember the fire triangle? Well, much like too little oxygen will make it hard to light a fire, too much oxygen can make your fire burn more quickly than you would like. Close the air-valve levers (including the damper), so that they're only open about one-third of the way.

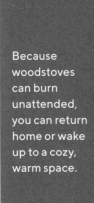

Because woodstoves can burn unattended, you can return home or wake up to a cozy, warm space.

Unlike fireplaces or campfires, woodstoves can safely burn unattended, with the appropriate maintenance and attention. A good rule of thumb is to empty the ashes daily (or with every use), clean the inside of the stove weekly, and have your chimney cleaned annually.

Keeping a fire going overnight can keep a home cozy and warm and make the morning just a little less difficult, as some woodstoves will still have embers to relight the next morning. Before you head off to bed, you'll want to really ramp the fire up. Here's how: open the air valves again, add larger pieces of hardwood to the fire, and let them get going for about twenty-five minutes. Then close the valves back down again to where they were before. This movement of the valves increases the flow of oxygen to the flames and then tamps it back down so that the fuel in the stove burns a bit more slowly.

7

Fire Safety

—————— ✕ ——————

Extinguishing a Fire
Indoors and Out

> *"Man is the only creature that dares to light a fire and live with it. The reason? Because he alone has learned to put it out."*

Henry Jackson Vandyke, Jr.

Y ou've enjoyed hours near your campfire or fireplace, soaking up the warmth and watching flames grow and recede, fan, and fade away. It's time for bed and, because you'll no longer be tending the fire, time to put it out. Any time you leave the fire, whether for bed, a starlit walk, or a morning hike, be sure to extinguish it properly. Escaped campfires can lead to major wildfires, and it doesn't take long. Improperly-cared-for woodstoves and fireplaces are responsible for burning down countless homes every year.

Which, of course, isn't to say don't have a fire! But do be prepared and take proper care to both light and extinguish your fires properly.

OUTDOORS

A significant part of proper fire management comes at the beginning of the process. Don't forget the tips from previous sections about building smaller fires rather than larger ones; keeping your fire away from tinder both below and overhead; avoiding oily-poppy wood, like pine, which can send out hot embers many feet from your fire; and never leaving a fire unattended.

When it comes time to extinguish your campfire, think back to the fire triangle. You'll have to remove at least one of the key ingredients to hinder the reaction. In the case of most fires, oxygen is the easiest element to remove. And, when it comes to campfires, that means "drowning" your fire. This is most easily accomplished if your fuel (logs) has already burned almost all the way to ash. But it still requires some work. A fire that burns for around three hours can be up to five hundred degrees Fahrenheit.

In one experiment, a fire that burned for three hours was left to burn and then monitored. Eight hours later the fire that burned without being extinguished at all was still one hundred degrees Fahrenheit. That's hot enough to severely burn you, and fires can easily reignite, which poses the threat of wildfire.

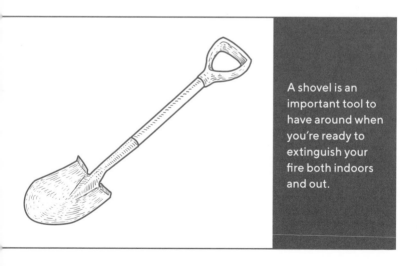

A shovel is an important tool to have around when you're ready to extinguish your fire both indoors and out.

BURNS

Playing with fire, as we all know, leads to increased risk of burns. While burns can be managed or avoided entirely with the appropriate precautions, they still happen. And knowing how to treat them is an important backcountry skill.

For major (third-degree) burns, medical help will be required, and some of the treatments below do not apply. For minor and moderate burns (first- and second-degree) that you can treat, start by placing the burned area under cool water. Flush rather than emerge the burn for five minutes to remove the heat from the tissue. Don't use ice, which can cause further damage to the skin. Burned areas can swell quickly, so be sure to remove any jewelry or tight clothes. Next you'll want to use clean water to gently wash the area before loosely wrapping the burn in dry gauze. Burns are prone to infection, so be sure the material you use is sterile. Ibuprofen, acetaminophen, and naproxen can all be used to help alleviate the pain from burns.

To properly extinguish a fire, begin by sprinkling it with water. Then, using a stick or shovel, stir the moistened ash and embers together. Pour more water over the fire and stir again. Continue repeating this process until you can hold your hand just barely above the embers and not feel heat. As a general rule, if the fire is too hot to touch, it's also too hot to leave behind.

If you are in a water-scarce environment and packing your own water, you can use sand or soil to suffocate your fire as well. You'll want to take extra precautions with this method as it doesn't work as well as using water, and embers buried beneath the surface can smolder for days.

In the same experiment I mentioned above, the fire that was covered in sand was also still nearly one hundred degrees eight hours after it was "extinguished." Campfires that are covered with sand pose the additional danger of being disguised by their sandy top, which can be especially dangerous if you're camping with children.

Water, on the other hand, cooled the fire to less than fifty degrees in just ten minutes. After eight hours, it was only ten degrees.

INDOORS

When you put out a fire in your fireplace or woodstove, you'll employ the same rules of the equation, and in most cases, oxygen is still the simplest ingredient to remove. That being said, the tools are different. Where backpacking and camping call for lightweight tools and sometimes limited supplies, the same isn't (or doesn't have to be) true in your home.

Much like a campfire, the most effective way to put out a fireplace fire is using water. Once your fire has burned down and smoldering black embers and ash are all that remain, use a spray bottle or other container to pour or mist water over the fire. Then, using a poker or other heatproof stick, stir the ashes around to distribute the moisture. Spray and stir again.

The second method involves much the same procedure, but instead of water, you'll use baking soda. Before spreading the baking soda over the fire, you'll want to use a fire poker to spread the remaining wood and embers out so that they're as flat as possible. Using a small shovel, scoop ash and spread it over the flames until there are none visible. Next, sprinkle the fire and embers with baking soda until they're covered in a fine coating. If the fire restarts, go back to the ash step and repeat, then repeat the baking soda step until the fire no longer relights.

After several hours (plenty of time for the ashes to cool), you can scoop the ashes into a metal container. Don't worry too much about larger chunks of wood—they'll burn the next time you light up a fire. Caution: never dump ashes into cardboard, plastic, or paper. Heat from the ashes or buried embers could burn through these materials and leave a burn on your floor or counter or, worst-case scenario, start a fire in your home.

Woodstoves are a bit more difficult to put out than fireplaces or camp stoves. But when it comes to putting out a fire in your woodstove, the design of the stove itself comes in handy. By closing the valves, you can deprive the fire of oxygen. This can, however, lead to creosote buildup in your chimney. In an ideal world, you can let the fire burn down and cool naturally.

If you need to put out a woodstove fire quickly, the baking soda method used for fireplaces can also work. Water works, too, but it can make a mess of the ashes and render them a sort of cement putty that's difficult to remove.

If you must remove a fire from a woodstove for one reason or another (say, there is a chimney fire, or your home is filling with smoke and you can't figure out why), you can also place the burning logs into a metal bucket and take them outside. You'll want to wear gloves and use the appropriate fire tools. And be sure to have a fire extinguisher nearby in case some of the logs or embers fall onto carpet or something flammable. Obviously, this method isn't ideal, but in a pinch it can work.

THE UNWELCOME FIRE AND HOW TO EXTINGUISH IT

Not all fires are planned or welcome. But much like being prepared to extinguish a runaway campfire or woodstove is an important skill, so is being prepared to battle less expected (and sometimes less intuitive) fires. Here are a few tips for having the right tools on hand and taking the right approach to handling dangerous fires.

EXTINGUISHING A GREASE FIRE

While most common in the kitchen, grease fires can occur anywhere that grease does (think campfire, grill, etc.). And, while your first instinct may be to hurl water at the flames, don't. In the case of grease on fire in a pan, any water you dump on it sinks to the bottom of the pan and then evaporates, essentially exploding and spreading flaming oil in the process. Without water as an option, consider your best alternatives to remove one of the three fire ingredients. First, remove any source of heat (turn off the oven or grill, for example). If the fire is small enough, consider placing a lid over the fire to cut off the oxygen supply. A word of caution about this approach: in one account that I read, a gentleman threw the lid on a flaming pot and, not seeing any more flames, thought the fire was out. He lifted the lid, and the influx of oxygen caused the fire to flare up again rapidly, burning him badly. So, if you are successful at trapping the fire beneath a lid, be sure to wait until the fire and everything around it have adequately cooled before attempting to remove it. Depending on the size of the fire, you can also place a wet rag over the flames. Do

WHAT KIND OF EXTINGUISHER SHOULD I HAVE? AND HOW DO I USE IT?

You know the saying "A chain is only as strong as its weakest link." Well, the same is true when it comes to using this common household item, which, more often than not, gathers dust in forgotten corners of kitchens and garages. Having an extinguisher on hand is the first step; ensuring you have the right one and knowing how to use it (or them) are critical next steps.

There are a number of extinguishers on the market, and they vary greatly in price, size, and optimal uses. Extinguishers that use water are rare these days, which is a good thing for the most part, as they only made things like grease fires worse. CO_2 extinguishers are commonly available, and instead of trying to remove the heat source, they "suffocate" the fire by displacing oxygen. Their biggest drawback is that they disperse quickly, so quickly that they're virtually useless outdoors. Dry-powder extinguishers are another alternative. They function by separating oxygen away from the fuel source to smother the fire. But because they produce a powder, they work better outdoors and for kitchen or electrical fires. The downside: the powder leaves a mess indoors, and these extinguishers should be serviced annually, regardless of use.

It's not a bad idea to have both CO_2 and dry-powder extinguishers, keeping the dry powder in the kitchen.

Generally, fire extinguishers operate fairly similarly, but it's best to read the instructions and familiarize yourself with the exact type you've purchased. That being said, a rule of thumb is to use the PASS technique: **PULL** the pin to break the seal; **AIM** the nozzle at the base of the fire; **SQUEEZE** the handle slowly to release the extinguishing agent; and **SWEEP** the extinguisher from side to side until the fire is out. If the fire reignites after you've stopped, repeat the process.

If you're putting out a "normal fire" or a grease fire, stay a safe distance from the fire, aim at the base of the fire, and slowly move across the area. If you stand too close or squeeze the lever (discharge) too quickly, you can spread the fire by spraying it with the powerful jet of the extinguisher. If you're putting out an electrical fire, make sure that you've turned off the power (if it's safe to) and then direct the hose spray straight at the fire.

this only with small fires. A third alternative is to dump baking soda on the flames. Baking soda works by releasing carbon dioxide and suffocating the fire. But, much like the rag, a large-enough fire will not be quelled with baking soda. Salt, a fourth alternative, takes a different approach: it sucks heat out of the grease. The right fire extinguishers (like those described on pages 110 and 111) are a fifth option and perhaps the most effective, if used properly.

HOW TO PUT OUT AN ELECTRICAL FIRE

If a fireplace isn't your sole source of heat, it's likely that additional warmth is provided by electric baseboard or space heaters, both of which can cause electrical fires (and so can things like toaster ovens and hair driers). When an electrical fire starts, the first step is to remove the heat/energy source by unplugging it (if you can safely do so). Then, as is true with a grease fire, baking soda can be used to squelch the flames. If the fire is small enough, baking soda will work to smother the flames. And like with grease fires, don't use water to put the fire out—you run the risk of being shocked or electrocuted in the process. If you aren't able to put the fire out, you need to shut the door to the room, leave your home immediately, and call 911 to avoid further risk of injury or death. As mentioned in the extinguisher section, electrical fires are a Class C fire, so any extinguisher you use must be "C" certified.

WAIT, DON'T BURN THAT!

We've spent a lot of time in this book covering what to burn and how to burn it. Not surprisingly, there is an inverse to that list—a number of materials that, when burned, can be toxic to both humans and the environment.

While this is not a comprehensive list, it should cover some of the most common items and remind you to double-check before burning anything other than untreated, dry, seasoned wood.

- The first thing to watch out for is treated wood. If you're burning old building supplies or scrap wood, be wary. Some wood is treated with toxic chemicals. As a rule of thumb, don't burn wood that has been pressure treated, painted, stained, or glued or has nails in it. Old wood or wood that has been exposed to moisture can also be contaminated with mold, which can be released into the air upon burning.

- While some plant matter makes great tinder, others can cause harm to your respiratory system. You may be familiar with plants like poison ivy, poison oak, and poison sumac. They all contain urushiol, an oil that causes an allergic reaction when touched. In addition to making your skin break out in a terrible rash, these plants excrete the offending oil when burned and can cause a harmful allergic reaction in your mouth and lungs. Even if you don't burn the poison ivy or oak directly, be wary of wood that has come in contact with the plants as it can carry urushiol as well.

- Avoid junk mail, magazines, wrapping paper, and colored print media in general. The ink and chemicals used during the paper-making process mean these products (especially when burned inside) can be toxic.

- As mentioned in the fire starter chapter, dryer lint is another potentially dangerous fuel, as it can be composed of all kinds of things picked up from clothing or used in laundry detergent or fabric softener.

- Charcoal makes for great grilling and is safe to use in outdoor, well-ventilated areas. But never use charcoal in home fireplaces, as it produces carbon monoxide when burned.

- Burning garbage (including plastic), whether in your home fireplace or campfire, is dangerous business. The range of materials you might toss together can combine under heat to form toxic chemicals, and you don't know what kind of pollutants might form. Dioxin is one of the most common pollutants produced by burning plastics and driftwood (see below). Dioxin decomposes very slowly—once it enters the environment or your body, it sticks around for a while. It's both hormone-disrupting and cancer-causing, and it remains in soil, water, and crops as well.

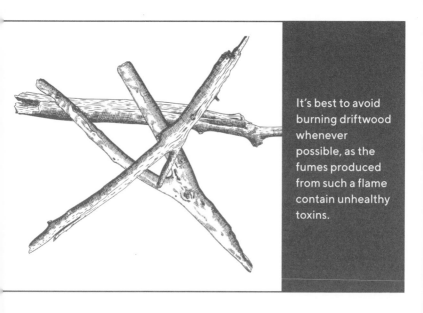

It's best to avoid burning driftwood whenever possible, as the fumes produced from such a flame contain unhealthy toxins.

In addition to harming yourself and the environment, burning garbage and plastic can cause irreparable damage to your fireplace or woodstove.

Depending on where you're camping, driftwood might seem like the perfect fuel for your fire; it's dry, light, and easily gathered. But driftwood poses a suite of health problems associated with its composition and what happens when it burns. If you've ever burned driftwood, you know that it can produce beautiful blue and lavender flames. But while attractive, those flames are toxic. The combustion of salt-soaked wood produces a lot of dioxin, which, as mentioned above, is toxic and stays around awhile.

SMOKE MANAGEMENT

If you've spent much time around a campfire, you've likely heard all sorts of strange, whispered spells that are said to send smoke in another direction. One of the most common that I've heard is "white rabbits," though other iterations include "fuzzy bunny" and "black rabbit." And, while I won't claim for certain that these don't work, here are some additional tips for managing smoke both indoors and out.

One important thing to remember is that smoke isn't good for you. The particles in smoke can, over time, lead to a number of negative health impacts, so properly managing smoke isn't just about convenience or preventing stinging eyes.

Indoors, you can minimize the impacts of smoke by having modern, efficient equipment and having your chimney cleaned regularly. Both indoors and out, burning only dry wood will help to reduce the smoke (don't burn wet, green, or pressure-treated wood; plastic;

garbage; dryer lint; or other materials). Don't burn debris (like leaves or grass) indoors and only use them to light your campfire. Don't use them as a continuing source of fuel (unless, of course, it's a matter of survival). And finally, allow proper airflow. The better you've built your fire, the less smoke you should have to deal with.

FOREST CLOSURES AND FIRE BANS

As many as 90 percent of wildfires in the United States are caused by humans. Whether you're camping or planning a backyard BBQ, it's always important to know about and follow local fire restrictions or bans. Before camping, visit the website of the appropriate land management agency to find out about restrictions.

Epilogue

Fire was, and continues to be, one of the most dynamic and transformational forces of all time. We are drawn to its warmth and function and intrigued by its capacity to both create and destroy. Sit around any campfire, and you'll watch as people—and likely you yourself—become mesmerized by the flames.

Our fascination with fire stems from a deep, biological desire to create and contain it. Some evolutionary anthropologists argue, in fact, that because fire has been so crucial to human survival for

Sitting before a campfire in the great outdoors is always a mesmerizing experience, no matter the occasion.

around a million years, our fascination with fire is directly linked to the fact that we didn't master fire as children, as people did historically (and, in some cultures, still do today).

But whatever the reason for our curious attraction to flame, mastering fire is the key to a unique kind of satisfaction that stems from being self-sufficient, harboring the ability to create something (even when the odds aren't in your favor), and providing for the ones you care about. With a healthy knowledge of fire you can create warmth, make food, usher in light, fend off cold or predators, purify water, signal for help, and continue to feel more deeply connected to something central to our way of life.

Firewood BTU Ratings for Common Tree Species

The BTU ratings that follow let you compare different firewood types and determine the best wood for your needs.

These charts provide the amount of energy per cord of wood for some of the most common firewood species. There is often conflicting data between different sources due to different variables used in the calculations, such as how much actual solid wood is assumed to be in a cord. A cord is 128 cubic feet, but in any stack of wood there will be air space between the pieces. As a result, a cord may have only seventy to ninety cubic feet of actual solid wood. This varies with the size and shape of the wood and how tightly it is stacked.

WESTERN HARDWOODS

(figures from the California Energy Commission BTU ratings, based on ninety cubic feet of solid wood per 128-cubic-foot cord)

	Heat Content, in millions of BTUs per cord	Weight, pounds per cord (green)	Weight, pounds per cord (dry)
Live Oak	36.6	7870	4840
Eucalyptus	34.5	7320	4560
Almond	32.9	6980	4350
Pacific Madrone	30.9	6520	4086
Dogwood	30.4	6520	4025
Oregon White Oak	28.0	6290	3710
Tanoak	27.5	6070	3650
California Black Oak	27.4	5725	3625
Pepperwood (Myrtle)	26.1	5730	3450
Chinquapin	24.7	4720	3450
Bigleaf Maple	22.7	4940	3000
Avocado	20.8	4520	2750
Red Alder	19.5	4100	2600
Quaking Aspen	18.0	3880	2400
Cottonwood	16.8	3475	2225

(chart contains some common nonnative species)

WESTERN SOFTWOODS

(figures from the California Energy Commission BTU ratings, based on ninety cubic feet of solid wood per 128-cubic-foot cord)

	Heat Content, in millions of BTUs per cord	Weight, pounds per cord (green)	Weight, pounds per cord (dry)
Western Larch (Tamarack)	28.7	5454	3321
Douglas Fir	26.5	5050	3075
Western Juniper	26.4	5410	3050
Western Hemlock	24.4	5730	2830
Port Orford Cedar	23.4	4370	2700
Lodgepole Pine	22.3	4270	2580
Jeffrey Pine	21.7	4270	2520
Ponderosa Pine	21.7	4270	2520
Sitka Spruce	21.7	4100	2520
White Fir	21.1	3190	2400
Red Fir	20.6	4040	2400
Coast Redwood	20.1	4040	2330
Grand Fir	20.1	3880	2330
Incense Cedar	20.1	3880	2350
Sugar Pine	19.6	3820	2270

EASTERN HARDWOODS

(figures compiled from various sources)

	Heat Content, in millions of BTUs per cord	Weight, pounds per cord (dry)
Osage Orange	32.9	4728
Shagbark Hickory	27.7	4327
Eastern Hornbeam	27.1	4016
Black Birch	26.8	3890
Black Locust	26.8	3890
Blue Beech	26.8	3890
Ironwood	26.8	3890
Bitternut Hickory	26.5	3832
Honey Locust	26.5	4100
Apple	25.8	3712
Mulberry	25.7	4012
Beech	24.0	3757
Northern Red Oak	24.0	3757
Sugar Maple (Hard Maple)	24.0	3757
White Oak	24.0	3757
White Ash	23.6	3689
Yellow Birch	21.8	3150
Red Elm	21.6	3112
Hackberry	20.8	3247
Kentucky Coffeetree	20.8	3247
Gray Birch	20.3	3179
Paper Birch	20.3	3179

	Heat Content, in millions of BTUs per cord	Weight, pounds per cord (dry)
White Birch	20.2	3192
Black Walnut	20.0	3120
Cherry	20.0	3120
Green Ash	19.9	2880
American Elm	19.5	3052
Black Cherry	19.5	2880
White Elm	19.5	3052
Sycamore	19.1	2992
Black Ash	18.7	2924
Red Maple (Soft Maple)	18.1	2900
Box Elder	17.9	2797
Catalpa	15.9	2482
Aspen	14.7	2295
Butternut	14.5	2100
Willow	14.3	2236
American Basswood	13.5	2108
Cottonwood	13.5	2108

EASTERN SOFTWOODS

(figures compiled from various sources)

	Heat Content, in millions of BTUs per cord	Weight, pounds per cord (dry)
Rocky Mountain Juniper	21.6	3112
Eastern Larch (Tamarack)	20.8	3247
Jack Pine	17.1	2669
Norway Pine	17.1	2669
Pitch Pine	17.1	2669
Black Spruce	15.9	2482
Hemlock	15.9	2482
Balsam Fir	14.3	2236
Eastern White Pine	14.3	2236
Eastern White Cedar	12.2	1913